T H E
BIG
C O N N E C T

SHAILI CHOPRA

RANDOM HOUSE INDIA

Published by Random House India in 2014

1

Copyright © Shaili Chopra 2014

Random House Publishers India Private Limited
Windsor IT Park, 7th Floor
Tower-B A-1, Sector-125
Noida 201301, UP

Random House Group Limited
20 Vauxhall Bridge Road
London SW1V 2SA
United Kingdom

ISBN 978 81 8400 550 9

Typeset in Minion Pro by Saanvi Graphics, Noida

Printed and bound in India by Replika Press Private Limited

Contents

1

Introduction

'These days, social media waits for no one. If you're LATE for the party, you'll probably be covered by all the noise and you might not be able to get your voice across. It could only mean that if you want to be heard by the crowd, you have to be fast; and on social media, that means you have to be REALLY fast.'

Aaron Lee (@askaaronlee)

In this new era, every tweet counts. Every view can be broadcast to the public at the click of a button. Social media has changed the way people think, write, and react. The desire for instant gratification coupled with the availability of networking platforms, or 'venting outlets' as I call them, at your fingertips, has created voracious digital hunger. A common man or woman now feels empowered as they have a voice to express their opinions. Social media is defined exactly as you'd think—a media for the society; for people to get more social and start a conversation. Whether it's a thought, an opinion, a picture, a video, a quote you read somewhere—you can easily share what's on your mind with your network. For artistes, social media allows an interactive platform to gauge feedback in a matter of seconds. Everyone from politicians to actors, editors to opinionators—a lethal

combination of opinion makers and opinion terminators—
are virtually present and far more accessible than in real
life. You can catch the pulse (and the impulse) of the public
right here and pretty quickly. For anyone wanting to read the
sentiment of people, the notion of a dipstick survey has been
replaced by a tweet-stick survey.

While our 'social fingertips' are new, less than a decade
old, '*being social*', of course, is an age-old idea. The social
networks which people were familiar with before the wired
networks arrived were aggregating in a town squares, going
door to door to spread a message in a neighbourhood,
blowing a trumpet to gather a group, public meetings for
fixing a problem or a town hall to discuss leadership. Today
the approach to campaigning in any election, championing
any social cause, or seeking opinion has similarly moved
to new platforms. Digital strategies are central to planning
political rallies and elections. Party manifestos are no longer
conspiracies of a coterie but laid bare in public eye. Canvassing demands a party's interactive presence on social platforms like Twitter, Facebook, Pinterest, YouTube, Google Plus
and others. The public, once the outsiders, are now privy
to a party's thought process. There is very little room to
bungle up as every enunciation is analysed and commented
upon. Politics today isn't just about getting elected. It's also
about getting *socially elected*. We've moved beyond just the
traditional rallies, tents, hordes of people, naarebaazi, boom
box speeches that surrounded every election. The promise of
people online, their social endorsement, is what parties jostle
for. Politicians are aware that they now must gratify people in
both real and virtual worlds.

Social media connects people, gets them talking and
sharing; allows campaigners to know the voters, target

specific audience, splice demographics, mobilize support, and urge them to participate. When some of these people, otherwise part of the audience, get actively engaged in political debates, they become a great tool to spread the word and influence opinion. There will be about 149 million first-time voters in 2014. Majority of the first-time voters belong to a demographic to whom technology comes easy. Assuming that a significant chunk of these voters belong to urban India, then they can easily be targeted through social media. So for example, if the difference in votes between the Congress and BJP was just 40 million, could the Internet brigade be urged, provoked, inspired, and encouraged to bridge this gap? In the last election the number of people who voted in favour of Congress exceeded the BJP by 40 million. So this 40 million added to the fresh voters coming to polls, are now the big focus of the social media campaigns. Can social media influence these voters? The answer may not be an unequivocal yes, but it certainly isn't a no. It's an answer in progress.

Irrespective of campaigning and hash tag wars, the real impact of technology has been in sensitizing and popularizing voter registration among the youth. Politicians who are on social media have a better connection to their potential or existing audience than those who aren't. Social media grants the power to lead, to follow. It even has the power to bring about change. There is no doubt that social media has become a pervasive force of impact and influence. However, a post, pin, or tweet doesn't necessarily translate into a vote. So the question is how much sway does social media actually hold in politics? How much influence do the trio of Facebook, Twitter, and Linkedin have on voters' opinions, analysis, and ideas exchange? As an active denizen of the tweeting class, I saw an opportunity in exploring the role of social media right before a pivotal election. This book explores the impact social media is having not only to influence communication in general but also changing the way politicians are using specific tools to reach out to their electorate. At a time mainstream media is going by whats trending on Twitter, leaders realize the clout a simple post can have.

But there are more fundamental questions to answer. As these social avenues bring out the political best in some people, will it pull them out of their slumber and take them to voting booths? Can the online charisma of politicians backed by a dogged pursuit of converting them into votes—through a contingent of volunteers—give democracy a new chance?

That social media is changing the world's consumption of information, of that there is no doubt but is this the best way forward? Twitter and Facebook are like countries online given their scale and size. How wrong can people and organizations be investing time, money, and leadership in communities online? Social media as a concept remains resonant with people as networking websites have become an extension of who we really are. This generation, especially, has been brought up in a world of hyper-communication. Which means social platforms are an excellent place to engage young and urban—who are rarely seen at Indian political rallies—voters. The figure that can change the game—37 percent of the urban Indian voters are online according to a Google survey. Nearly 4 out of every 10 urban voters in India are on the Internet, a little less than the 42 percent that are undecided about who they will vote for in the 2014 general elections, according to a survey by Google India and research agency TNS released in October 2013.

Gujarat Chief Minister Narendra Modi tweets to talk. At a friend's wedding, BJP leader Arun Jaitley selects a corner to keep up with his Facebook timeline and gives his nods as 'likes' to friends and followers. Sanjay Jha, spokesperson for the Congress, is live on Twitter when he isn't on television. It's the first time in Indian history that the Indian National Congress, Aam Aadmi Party, and even the Bharatiya Janata Party have seeked suggestions from social media followers on their manifestoes. Such changes like crowdsourcing a draft plan on how to run a country, electioneering, and interacting with the voters goes miles in trumpeting a change in the new communication order of the world's largest democracy.

So one wonders, given the wide-reaching impact social media is having, can it spur a revolution in politics like it has in civil society? Can an Arab Spring like online success bear fruit and bring political outcomes in a country like India? Can it take lounger thought-leaders head to cast votes and make effective their voice on Twitter and Facebook? Can the discourse and debate around the digital generation actually urge them to participate in the democracy rather than simply enjoying its gifts of freedom of expression? The higher turnout during state elections in late 2013 is encouraging, but it can't be attributed to social media alone. However, it did cement the notion that campaigning via social media and connecting people online paid off for politicians when combined with a strong website and donation drive. Take the case of the Aam Aadmi Party which derives its entire volunteer strength from social media, which in turn is then collected to act on the ground. Other traditional political parties like Congress and BJP are trying the other route by converting their on-ground successes and work into building digital edifices that will leverage upon history and legacy to induce online interest. There is no one method that can guarantee votes; but a strategic plan for the online public is better than no online presence at all. Experiments can work. New thinking is welcome. Today this open-mindedness to new concepts and approaches is also a byproduct of social media suffusing our lives—social lives, political lives, and economic lives.

What India is witnessing today, the United States saw 5 years ago, when in 2008, Barack Obama stood against the formidable power and combined charm of the Clintons and won. Obama's A team adopted social media and data analytics, analysed social media barometers, and crafted ideas to appropriate media from Facebook to Twitter to public forums in 2012. Even Mitt Romney was forced to announce his presidential run on Twitter in just 140 letters. It's amazing how social media has made icons of newbies, produced new election experts, announced candidature, declared poll results, exposed politicians, and even brought many down.

While India and United States are using social media for political mileage, social revolutions have fermented from the Internet's new found power. Social media has bound people together in a common voice with a familiar goal—whether these are flash protests outside the World Economic Forum in Davos, the uprising we now call Arab Spring which includes the groundbreaking wave in Libya, expression of oppression in Egypt, or even the protest and public mobilization against the 16 December, 2012 gang-rape, and the Anna Hazare movement of India Against Corruption closer home. Some of these events may not have been triggered by social media but it made online networks its arms and legs to run campaigns, spread the word, and connect like-minded people. It helped in shaping the final outcome in terms of protest and meeting points. What surely can't be ignored is the ability of social media to bring together common interest groups on political, social, or moral causes.

As social media expands, as outcomes are scientifically understood and analysed, what will take precedence over self-perpetrated popularity and like-meters is the ability of social media to have an *impact on impact*. Kristen Purcell, the research director at Pew Internet Society in America says, 'What they really want is to have impact. Most have felt proud of a group they belong to in the past year and just under half say they accomplished something they couldn't have accomplished on their own.'[1]

Monumental changes brought upon by social media deserve to be scrutinized and hailed. What role does social media play in political campaigns? Why engaging is more important than informing? Can likes be votes? Are politicians still deluded by the notion that this is a toy and not a tool? As it has been seen, though it removes the flab of middlemen, it also exposes politicians directly to their voters. Openness invites criticism. The bottom line is that the rules of the game of winning elections have officially changed. Social media is here to stay. If leaders want to win elections, they ought to be in the place where people are—and that's online—making choices, liking, disliking, and listening to their friends rave or rant against their political choices.

Reference

1. http://pewinternet.org/Reports/2011/The-Social-Side-of-the-Internet.aspx

2

How Social Media Impacts Politics

'Social media spark a revelation that we, the people, have a voice, and through the democratization of content and ideas we can once again unite around common passions, inspire movements, and ignite change.'
— Brian Solis, *Engage: The Complete Guide for Brands and Businesses to Build, Cultivate, and Measure Success in the New Web*

When political parties get down to conducting social media workshops as part of their business plan for elections, you know they are serious about this newly discovered digital story. The concept of meetings in bare rooms, laid with thick, white bedspreads and bolsters, where leaders would ruminate over party matters in darbar style, are old-fashioned ideas threatened by new-fangled networking tools. Google hangouts, Skype calls, and Facebook groups are where the brainstorming happens now. Social media meetings and conferences have come as a cultural break—adding zest to electioneering and, no doubt, to strategy planning. Politicians armed with smart phones are a common sight now, and they often tweet while at public events. Social media and new technology tools have gripped politicians who were only used to secretaries taking calls on their behalf. Now the added curiosity of the medium has leaders tweeting non-stop, sharing pictures of their visits and engaging with voters and people online, all this as an added dimension to traditional politics. India's government bodies are suddenly waking up to the magic of the *viral* and learning ways to disseminate news more effectively. According to ComScore's latest report, India has the world's third largest Internet population which overtook Japan's by adding 17.6 million users in the last year.[1] This has sparked some new thinking around how social media can change the way we consume politics.

National leaders, election candidates, and official government organizations are now active on social networking sites, a step beyond just being online through websites. In India while some individual leaders have had a first mover advantage, the government has also tried to play catch up, at least by using new media as an extension of their daily business. Prime Minister (PM) Manmohan Singh is on social networking site Facebook and on Twitter as @PMOIndia. Both these accounts are recurrently updated with political and national updates. Planning Commission has had a website for a while, and has also debuted on Facebook. The deputy chairman of the Commission discussed his 12th plan outlook on a Google hangout, making it a first in the history of the government body. Political parties such as Congress, Aam Aadmi Party, BJP, Samajwadi Party are all on Twitter. Narendra Modi, Arvind Kejriwal, Arun Jaitley, Sushma Swaraj, Shashi Tharoor, Jay Panda, Akhilesh Yadav, Manish Tewari, Ajay Maken are some leaders connected to people through tweets. Some are more active than the others while most use social media to share information, rally locations, and give reactions to news. Rajesh Lalwani of Blogworks says, 'Parties like the BJP and Aam Aadmi Party would appear slightly better organized on this medium, with larger support groups, but national parties like the Indian National Congress and others have also started to understand the impact and are beginning to enter the space quite aggressively.'

There is no doubt that use of social media by government or political outfits is a quick way to share information, and a cost effective platform for discussions and engagement with the country's citizens. Information technology advisor to the PM, Sam Pitroda, admits that there is a pressing need to leverage new media and possibly use it to find appropriate economic solutions. 'Today, as a nation of a connected billion, a first in the history of the world, we need to leverage emerging technologies, including social media, to help alleviate the enormous problem of poverty.'[2] Possibilities for using social media to improve government services are already coming into focus. As of now, the world over, web applications are emerging to offer citizens the option to report potholes, traffic challenges, connect with emergency services, women's safety and other problems when they encounter them. An initiative of a Bangalore based civil society organization, www.ipaidabribe.com has emerged as one of the key platforms to discuss corruption at all levels of government. Especially important has been its role in bringing to light rent seeking in the local government departments. They also have visibility on Facebook, Twitter, and YouTube that enables them to highlight corruption and empower common people by giving them a voice. A report from e-summit 2012 cites some other examples as well such as financial inclusion.[3] Social Media expert Vivek Wadhwa shares, 'People will use social networks that are special purpose, geared toward local communities, and in local languages. In parts of New Delhi, for example, localcircles. com is gaining popularity. It connects neighborhoods by allowing them to exchange information about water availability and domestic help; find blood donors; and report corruption. In China, Renren, Weibo, and Weixin — which have their own specialties — each have hundreds of millions of users.'4 The one way in which social media changes the political discourse is by offering itself as a tool for solutions. That Indian politicians and policy makers are becoming cognizant of such possibilities is itself a step in the right direction. It's an attempt to go beyond taking social media on its face value as an information disseminator and superimposing it to solving real problems of citizens.

As more and more people want to be 'part of' this solution, the power of social media is surfacing as a critical benchmark for change. In India, it was a turning point when Delhi was faced with its worst rape case event. In a widely reported incident, a woman was beaten and gang-raped in a private bus in which she was travelling with a male friend. There were six others in the bus, including the driver, all of whom raped the woman. The woman succumbed to her injuries and died thirteen days later while undergoing emergency treatment in Singapore. This incident shook the conscious of the Indian society like nothing in recent times. It questioned the structures and systems that lay the rules on women safety in India and as a consequence, there was public display of mass anger. The nation recorded a large number of rallies and protests on the streets, people creating pages on social media to highlight this incident, many voiced their thoughts through Twitter and Facebook, connected at public locations by coordinating through social media, the government was forced to respond to social media groundswell and take action. 'Nirbhaya' was the top trend on Twitter India and people across the world expressed shock, disgust, and demanded reforms in safety for women in India. This triggered more than a few dozen apps made for women's safety such as 'Guardian,' Nirbhaya—Be Fearless, FightBack, On Watch and many others. Global IT giant Microsoft came out with an app aimed at protecting women. According to an interview to PTI by the India head Raj Biyani, to use Guardian effectively, users need to add the names of friends, family members, and security groups to the settings and in an emergency situation, the app can be used to alert them, via the SOS button. All the user has to do is tap the SOS button.

'The phone then sends a distress SMS to all buddy mobiles, notifying them of the emergency along with location details. At the same time the SOS button also sends emails to buddy email IDs and posts to private Facebook groups, if registered,' Biyani explained.[5]

The massive awareness and the outrage against lack of safety measures across India forced several out of the box ideas. Sangeeta Makkad, professor of Media studies at Lala Lajpat Rai College in Mumbai along with her students created a Facebook page that helped them garner tremendous traction. Seeti Bajao was a campaign that asked women to whistle (seeti) when they were in trouble and used social media to make public aware of the idea.

Social media was central to connecting, networking, and bringing awareness among people in the aftermath of the rape case.

In a column for Forbes, Kiran Subbaraman of IBM highlights how this agitation and debate on social media eventually influenced the movement and made the Government re-look at some of its policies around protecting women in India.[6]

The Nirbhaya case was sort of a watershed in use of social media. And this incident even impacted the politics of the nation and most certainly the politics of the national capital. Sheila Dikshit, the three-term chief minister under Congress, was criticized for not doing more towards creating a safe environment for women in Delhi. One wonders how far this impacted the poor showing of Congress in the state election in Delhi.

Powerful as this wave of discontent was, this is only one example. There are several instances of using social media to garner support, drawing people together, holding public posts, and reaching out to the citizens. The Aam Aadmi Party and Anna Hazare's India Against Corruption movement both rejected the traditional corridors of power and are social media led. To a great extent, the rise of Narendra Modi remains a social media phenomenon. The leader has hardly had any mainstream media exposure sparing the last two years and continued to manifest his popularity via direct channels like social media. There are hundreds of case studies on what engrossed people on social media over the last few years. The hanging of 26/11 terrorist Ajmal Kasab, the massive power grid failure where 30 million people were without electricity in North India, the grounding of Kingfisher Airlines which triggered chaos for travellers as the carrier went bust, speeches and rallies by Rahul Gandhi and Modi giving way to hashtag wars, Rahul Gandhi's first TV interview, corruption scams, land laws, cyclones, the report of the Indian soldier who was mutilated after a gunfight with Pakistan, the Uttaranchal flash floods, Sarabjit's death in Pakistan surging Indian anger, Maoism and internal security challenges, L.K. Advani quitting BJP, and many other episodes of importance to the nation—

all found their way to social media for news flow and for reactions.

POLITICS AND SOCIAL MEDIA WORKSHOPS

The last few years have showcased the power of social media through the widespread exchange between people of India about causes, issues, debates, and politics. It has had the effect of extracting the political bone in every citizen. It's given every Twitter handle and Facebook user the power of opinion and expression. From a political standpoint, the example of the American elections shed light on how social media helps people make political choices. That social media mattered. In 2008, there were about 1.5 million election-related tweets within the US and across the world. By 2012, there were 31 million.[7] In India, too, we are seeing some trends like the US. In India, the population engaged in social media has risen over the last 24 months. According to the ComScore Survey cited above, 25 percent of all time spent online in India is dedicated to use of social media, compared to 33 percent in Russia and 38 percent in Brazil. The rising interest of Indians in social media has got politicians sitting up and taking notice because a majority of those on Twitter, Facebook, Orkut, and other streams are people below the age of 35, as per the same survey. Engaging with this demographic will be central to any political strategy in the country.

Seeing these trends, political parties have been forced to raise their social media skills to join the digital spree. In August 2013, Congress organized its first formal effort towards such 'social upliftment' and gathered its state and national leaders under one roof to understand and strategize the party's social media voice. The BJP, led by Narendra Modi, too conducted a programme in Delhi to make his party co-workers aware of the digital avenues for campaigning, as the leader believes this section of voters is desperate for change. BJP followed it up with regional workshops and conferences. In Chandigarh, for example, BJP's IT Cell boss Arvind Gupta said social media can be used to make fans and followers aware about 'the problems being faced by the countrymen and about the persons who are committed to solving these problems.'

In part, the idea behind these efforts by the two parties to educate leaders new to the idea of 140-characters on Twitter or just excited by the power of Facebook was so that they don't make complete fools of themselves.

For the Congress, a workshop led by the in-house communication experts of the party, such as Information and Broadcasting Minister Manish Tewari and Union Minister Shashi Tharoor, trained the participants on the 'dos and don'ts' of the 140-character social network—Twitter. However, it's hard not to bring up the fact that sometimes the doyens of social media teach by example. It's interesting to note that Shashi Tharoor was at the centre of a controversy even before his political colleagues could understand the concept of Twitter. In 2009, when he was the Minister of State for Human Resources, his tweet cost him his job. The government was driving an austerity campaign given the economic slowdown and had announced a slash in travel budgets for government servants. Finding humour in this idea, in a tweet, Tharoor said he would travel 'cattle class—out of solidarity with all our holy cows!' This was seen as elitist on one hand as twitterati wondered if he was ridiculing economy class passengers by alluding to 'cattle class', and being sarcastic about other politicians by calling them 'holy cows' on the other. Interpretations were left to trolls and opposition but the ruling party had to politely upset Tharoor over the matter. But that was then. Now, would it be safe to assume that political high-commands are more tolerant of Twitter and are familiar with controversial tweets?

Social media indeed carried seeds of change. And this change was becoming evident in the rising voice of the common man. Expression was at its peak on social media. Riding this wave was the Aam Aadmi Party (AAP). In 2012, AAP used social media in an unprecedented way with engagement and donation-seeking as their primary plan. AAP's young and energetic volunteer brigade used Facebook to convene meetings and set the agenda. They used Twitter to let loose new facts and ammunition against political rivals, and got people to donate online in a bid to introduce transparency. They multiplied their social media reach with actual tools rather than an intent and dependence on just volunteers. AAP experienced real benefits from social media which not only made people aware of their plans and agenda but also connected them with appropriate donors.

The example of AAP does highlight that social media isn't the self-flagellating bastion of a select few. It's not about just a bunch of journalists and news junkies following each other. Social media can be put to use to something more meaningful. It is being increasingly used to raise awareness for causes, to run campaigns, and as a place where people from all walks of life can gather and discuss the issues that they care about or would like to publicly criticize. Politicians are becoming cognizant of such changes. Some willingly and some by force.

The 2014 elections have a lot at stake. The Rath Yatras, the Chintan Shivirs, and the traditional political jamboree. But a new part of this strategy is to showcase ground activities, *online*. During all such events, political parties live tweet, and bring on-ground action to online denizens through posting and pinning. There is effort to analyse public sentiment, to mobilize support, and to get things trending. It's all happening in India and on timelines.

Political parties are slowly learning the nuances of the social media game. The hashtags are planned. The speeches are integrated for tweets. Politicians realize that suddenly thousands are speaking up; the general janta is now actively a part of the political mindshare or seeking it. A phone user with a camera is a journalist and any tweeter is a sort of a self-proclaimed editor. Social media is changing politics as we've seen through the ages. New columnists have emerged and writing has become the bastion of one and all. Arvind Gupta of the BJP IT Cell believes it's definitely setting a narrative and influencing a lot of people. Now people who use this are using it a lot more than they are watching TV or doing anything else. He says, 'Social media sets the narrative in two ways. One, because there are no intermediaries, and everyone has an equal chance to broadcast and influence, it allows for dissemination of all kinds of views without one single person or a group of people controlling the narrative. In such a fiercely competitive space therefore, only the better ideas survive the scrutiny. Second, the traditional influencers of the narrative, are almost all on social media. They read the same things and observe the same trends that any other person does. It thus influences the influencers too thereby creating another layer of influence.'

So does all this engagement and participation on social forum eventually benefit political parties? Can social media make them win elections? Can it bridge the divide between candidates and voters? It's a little bit of all of this. But for starters, it's a reflection of an entire society. 'I think it's less about what is the next nascent technology and it's more about how people's behaviour is changing—in the way they vote, in the way they purchase, in the way they communicate with each other,' elucidates Pete Snyder, founder and CEO of the Arlington-based social media firm New Media Strategies as quoted by *Politico*.[8]

In India, the impact of social media is still to be ascertained in a more defined way. We are driven by the syndrome where one takes the lead, the rest follow. So when Shashi Tharoor, self-styled social media personality, used it, hardly any other politician was on Twitter, and his cattle class tweet caused an uproar. Three years later, the very purpose of social media has become to create a stir, no matter how politically incorrect people may be. From politicians to public, everyone is taking on the other and creating more controversy.

THE OBAMA MODEL

Political parties in India are trying to replicate the Obama model of staying connected at all points via social media and other digital decisions. And this is not just limited to the use of the phrase 'Yes We Can' by Narendra Modi during his rallies. On his customized social network, mybarackobama. com, more than 2 millon people have created personal profiles and many of them interact to create infographics, set up events in their neighbourhoods, and even raise funds.[9] This is something being imbibed closely by the Aam Aadmi Party, which is new on the political scene and is trying to adopt transparent measures for raising funds to raise its public stature. Arvind Kejriwal, the founder of AAP, has often mentioned that they have been inspired by the Obama campaign and its use of technology.[10] Political parties are also trying to get people to register on their websites to ensure they are building a strong database of voters and supporters. In BJP's case, their website platform www.India272.com crowdsources party work to volunteers who register and put them to task to garner BJP support in their immediate locality. Obama during his campaign had used his website to empower other people to host fundraisers and campaign for him in their constituencies.

WHAT'S THE PERFECT STRATEGY?

In Obama's campaign, it's now well-documented that social media and technology were major success factors to develop a wave of empowered volunteers who felt they could make a difference. In India, this isn't true for most parties with the exception of AAP as explained earlier. Therefore, as it is the first time social media is playing such a big part on political parties' agendas, there is no clear digital business model, no one fixed social media strategy. There is, however, a tremendous amount of experimentation taking place.

As a result, it's worth going by a bit of precedence and some innovative thinking. Since there is no proven example of social media impacting votes but is most definitely hard to ignore, politicians are using multiple media strategies by setting up comprehensive tech divisions, social media teams, digital spokespersons, encouraging voluntary people to create satellite support group and contribute to the overall plan. No one, after all wanted to take the chance of putting all eggs in one basket.

So, what we have are multi-pronged agendas playing out simultaneously on this front. Let's look at the social media-agenda of any party. How is it planned and executed? First, political parties' core teams set the social agenda after discussing the impulses with the party leaders. Second, the communication is decentralized there on to volunteers and supporters who execute the umbrella plan. Third, the same is pushed out through social media where plenty of Twitter followers and Facebook friends of the party help take the information viral.

BJP's Arvind Gupta built a team of volunteers to spread the noise about the party's politics, views, and push instant reaction on newsbreaks. They have built a base of volunteers through their online outreach, who are well-informed about the party policy and its activities. He says, 'Volunteers connect to a political party in various ways. Traditional methods as well as technology enabled social media platforms both provide an opportunity for volunteers to associate with BJP. Social media has naturally been one of the most important platforms for BJP to build volunteer base.'

For Aam Aadmi Party, Arvind Kejriwal took the lead under the Anna revolution and now has support groups feeding into the party's on-ground activities via social media. Anna and Kejriwal certainly revolutionized the idea of mobilization through social media in India. Involving online audience has been a game changing tactic in the use of social media and its relevance to political rallies. This is especially true for the newbie party as it did not have established political tools from the past such as Rath Yatras (BJP) or Shivirs (Congress).

MAKING A FORMIDABLE STRATEGY

Simplyfy360's prescription

1. Decide and defend: Once on social media, be on it and defend why you believe in it. It is a time consuming exercise and needs understand and commitment. Fact is you cannot stay away from it in today's world so embrace it.

2. Understand the KPIs: Know what people expect from your social media strategy and work towards your audience. As political leaders, know what aspects and qualities your constituency expects of you. Being human, sensitive, intellectual, futuristic and being open minded are among the salient features people expect of their leaders.

3. Build an inclusive campaign: It should reach different part of the society, differently. Influential groups must be targeted.

4. Deliver with quality: put out the campaign with quality and keep it regular so you are engaged with your audience. Make content that creates impact. Be high on design and presentation. Use both content and design by putting out your posts at the right time.

5. Exploit the right channels: Use any of the media with a purpose and plan. Success cannot be incidental. Use social media across the board from Facebook, Pinterest to YouTube but understand which ones are promotional and which need engagement with a community.

6. Build an ecosystem: Talk less and listen more. Create buzz, put out reactions, showcase major leaders, put out regular reports, and post. Do it all.

7. Listen, Listen, Listen: Social media is about people. Let them talk and leaders role should be to listen.
8. Don't be a news broadcaster, be a newsmaker: You are a leader, people want to know what you have to say about critical things.
9. Making a strong online community: Winning lies on strength of building a big community.
10. Marry online and offline: Recognize social media as a medium and use to push forward your offline message.

BUDGET ALLOCATION

Use of social media has also become popular as it remains the most cost-effective tool. Once again this was an especially important factor for AAP, which began using it initially because they had no funds. 'Social media played an important role in AAP's success,' explains AAP's social media strategist Ankit Lal. 'Right from mobilizing people to sending across the correct information to people to countering the lies and confusion being spread by other parties, social media has proved to be an important tool.' But ever since these digital drives became successful for a few, all parties joined the bandwagon. No party wants to be left out. As a result some of them are paying or are carving teams to keep up social media accounts, advertising on networking and blogging websites, and making an annual budget for the same. With elections right here, and this general frenzy around social media, budget allocations for this space have skyrocketed and in some cases have become befogged with logic. How much does it cost to do a top of the line social media campaign? Do the campaigns target the correct audience? Flush with money and chasing algorithms, parties are certain that they must invest but don't know where to stop. Or for that matter, how much they should start with. There has been buzz about the Congress spending ₹100 crore in a campaign to proactively rebut the BJP. Sanjay Jha, Congress Spokesperson, rubbished this figure saying, 'The ₹100 crore social media budget is BJP's attempt at mathematical creativity; it is utter rubbish. Social media moves on exponential, spontaneous, and genuine involvement of people not on a forced multiplier created by paid staff, the model.' BJP's Gupta, on his part, explains that volunteers drive much of BJP's social media although they do have a 'small budget'. 'To run the party website, associated social media profile of official BJP platforms (BJP Twitter handle, FB page) and to run our Internet TV initiative—Yuva TV, we do have an IT team and associated small budget. Other than this we do not have any specific social media budget since the entire BJP presence on social media has been volunteer driven,' says Gupta.

Kejriwal's party has a ratio to go by, so about 2 to 3 percent of the total budget is spent on the party's outreach efforts online. In most cases, there are well-wishers, volunteers who take upon themselves the task of driving political campaigns from the outside of traditional boundaries. There are those faceless and identity-quiet organizations, companies that spend on political parties without declaring where the money is going. While India too is adding to coffers of social media firms, it's clearly nowhere as effective, transparent, analytical, or impact-driven as the Obama campaign. The Obama campaign spent $47 million on digital marketing. And the Romney campaign spent $4.7 million.[11] So did the difference on social media spending win Obama the election? Can budgets be directly correlated to winning streaks? That's an often-asked question in the aftermath of his win.

On their part, Indian political parties are doing all they can by setting up nodal agencies (both formal and informal) to disseminate information. Aam Aadmi Party has released apps on Android. These include lists of candidates by constituency, and videos and other content released by the party. BJP4India is another example of an app on Android. There was a recent controversy around two other apps purportedly done by the BJP called Shivraj App (after Shivraj Singh Chauhan of Madhya Pradesh) and a gaming application Modi Run (named after the popular game Temple Run). Opposition to these has been from the Congress for influencing voters.[12]

There is still debate on whether to devote a budget or not for social media. As Indian parties claim, they depend on volunteers to push for more spread. While that's surely one effective way, it also leaves them uncertain about the actual extent of the communication. Do they spend on getting likes and followers on Facebook and Twitter? If yes, then how is that strategy planned? A lot is yet unclear about how social media can expand campaigns. There is still a lot in the realm of the unknown as hit and try methods are in play.

WHAT DOES IT DO FOR PARTIES?

Social media is a great barometer of mood and an instant judge of the way people see any political, social, or economic development. It lays bare the views of the public, it exposes the chinks in the 'stated view' of things, allowing media and campaign strategists to use the fine cracks and inject their version of events, their counter views, alternate thinking, and convenient but factual research that suits their cause.

The increase in uptake of digital tools by political figures and parties and the direct access factor has got campaign planners reworking plans and redrawing conclusions. Such qualitative efforts are now being termed as 'sentiment analysis' tools. Social media is being used to do a litmus test of people's mood on key subjects for electioneering.

'Social media is influencing mainstream media discourse,' shares veteran journalist Ashok Malik. 'It is also making those politicians and public servants who use social media sensitive—even over-sensitive—to the opinions and complaints of those they interact with using social media. It is making symbolic and peripheral changes.'

Social media is also pulling in new people, as older generations take to the Internet phenomenon, and engaging with them. It's naïve to think that it's a tool for the young only. Many homemakers have gone to becoming opinion makers and influencers.

Social media is a brilliant tool for voter mobilization as seen in the case of the state elections in December, 2013. The state saw highest voter turnout witnessed in an election for the Delhi Assembly at 67 percent, much higher than 61.75 percent in 1993, the second highest ever recorded in post independence era. This is an example of how social media actually led people out to convert online conversations into an 'act of change'. Such mobilization is also very cost-effective. No armies of volunteers are needed while infrastructure and logistical costs are nearly zero. In America, for example, it's almost commonplace to have supporters at a rally check into Foursquare or Facebook, live-tweet the important highlights, have barcodes or digital entry, and quickly and automatically connect to the particular politician's website. In India, as well, the trends are progressively changing as now it's impossible to have a rally or a public political meeting without hashtag mentions which are shared with all. This book examines the idea of mobilizing people and the kind of activity needed to keep the flow of opinions strong till the very end.

That leaves us with the crucial question—do social media strategies convert into votes? History has it that Franklin D. Roosevelt used radio to change the way he governed while John F. Kennedy was successful in wooing television audience. Things moved online when Howard Dean saw the value of the Internet for raising money. Then came Barack Obama who added social media to these existing means. This networking tool helped him build his brand. In the Indian context, this may yet be a far-out idea although social media has become a vertebra for communication and campaigning. Social media platforms are likely to be influential in 160 of India's 543 Parliament constituencies, making Facebook and Twitter users the nation's newest voting bloc, according to a survey by Internet and Mobile Association of India.[13]

Social media is considered a solid space for debate and its impact on actual elections is still being studied. 'Important as these are, I would hesitate to call them substantial changes as of now. So there is a role, though probably not quite a material role,' asserts Malik. The pattern of usage of the social medium by political parties and leaders is likely to evolve as they start to understand the nature and value this phenomenon better in terms of ability to engage citizens. 'The value of data that social conversations throws up will help decipher mood, emerging and shifting themes, role of technology in scaling up, and micro-targeting and so on,' explains Rajesh Lalwani who runs Blogworks.

How social media is changing the game

- Connects people and generates massive traffic
- Leads to speedy and direct communication
- Communication can be creative, provocative, emotive, and interactive
- Strategists can use social media to target specific demographic groups, splice reach by interests, and produce intended communication
- It's a captive audience
- Is influential and allows for influencing an audience by appealing to them, their friends, acquaintances, and family
- Empowers people, turns them into information seekers, opinion makers, and gives them a sense of participation

RISE OF THE 'EXPERTS'

Social media analysis has pushed for a new breed of experts, many self-appointed and others who have displayed better knowledge of the platform within the polity. Qualitative analysis has allowed a new breed of experts to come forth who are primarily experts in adding 'shrill factor' taking pre-determined viewpoints, and adding spice to debates. Of course some of these reflections may well be their real views. The online debate is not for moderates. It's an extreme world out there. These are the ones driving the campaigns. The fence sitters are their targets.

THE MESSAGING TRANSFORMS

Political behaviour on each social network is different and must be custom-made for the platform. For example, all those spewing anger or taking sides on Twitter are unlikely to display their political affiliations on Linkedin, their professional space. Politics in India can get personal and most people do not like exposing their political leanings at the workplace or potential organizations.

At the same time, the general, 'face-less' and anonymous nature of social media allows people to share candid views without inhibition. On Twitter, communication is not intimate. You can reach and tag anyone you may or may not know, actively participate in discussions that are mostly open, and still remain anonymous by not using your real name as your handle. These are reasons why users are not that worried about how their tweets are perceived by others.

Facebook is a more closed platform where you are recognized and therefore your views are as well. People are aware that if they express a view, it's then known to people and that they want those friends/family to know what their view is in the first place. As Facebook mostly involves a mutual relationship before friends can see your timeline, it is an interesting space to bring together like-minded people. This also explains the surge of 'fan pages'. All political parties have used Facebook quite effectively to engage with a larger audience, instantly and in a widespread way. With 'fan pages', the engagement can also become a little more detached but at the same time carry all full-fledged features of Facebook interactivity.

There is a wide expectation that it's the people below 35 that need to actively participate in the country's future and cast their votes. The youth needs to remain in the electoral net to demand changes in regime and as a voice of new India. If that's the case, then social media appears to be an appropriate and indispensable tool. A report estimates that by June 2014, India will have 243 million Internet users, at which point of time, it is expected to overtake the US as the second largest Internet base in the world. China currently leads with more than 300 million Internet users while the US currently has estimated 207 million Internet users.[14]

So when politicians come knocking next for votes, here are the questions to address. Does your politician deserve your vote? Do you know enough about them? Are they engaging with you online? Is there a self-driven attempt at reaching out, redressing issues and then taking them offline for execution? If there is one significant impact that social media is having, it is in its transformation of politics and leadership behaviour. Shamiyana-covered public rallies where the politician sat on a pedestal and people (aka voters) sat beneath on the ground—this image of politics is most definitely changing, at least in urban India, where the voter has mostly been missing from polling booths. Historically, half of the urban population abstained from the elections and the rural voters accounted for the maximum part of the total voter turnout ratio. 2014 would be the first general elections in India where social media would play a large and perhaps impactful role. It promises to create peer pressure on the voters to cast their vote.

Reaching out to voters online is not only important, but it's essential. One can argue that if citizens are core to a democracy then social media has taken a long step in extending this democratic process. Social media has suddenly offered that intimacy, access and direct reach, which even television failed to attract. The digital medium is interactive. It's a form of engagement. This election is critical because according to the census conducted in 2011, India had 149.36 million first time voters who are expected to have a greater access to Internet and newer media.[15]

'Today, individuals have access to an unprecedented form of direct and interactive contact with people in positions of authority and this has created a strong sense, though derided by some as mostly illusory and superficial, of political empowerment,' says Shashi Tharoor who was, until recently, India's most followed politician on social media.[16]

At the end of the day, however, for any campaign to be successful, the message has to move beyond just likes, posts, and tweets. A political party needs votes. Social media is possibly more about the importance of people participating and less about self-promotion of political parties. It needs to carry an authentic message. But it's not enough to look at these changes and talk about social media as just a new platform. 'Social media is not just a change in technology; it is a change in how people communicate. This change has to be reflected in how candidates behave, not just online but everywhere' explains Dan Jeffers in Social Media Monthly.[17]

How Politicians Gain: Nitin Pai's prescription

Nitin Pai, director of the Takshashila Institute, spoke to the author and prescribed the following.

- They can engage the people directly—political leaders do not have to rely on media persons and even their own party bureaucracy in order to reach out to the people
- They can strengthen their leadership brand—by discussing important issues on a regular basis, political leaders can better project their image to the public

- They can listen to people—more savvy users of social media can understand public sentiment and pulse
- They can mobilize more efficiently—social media allows leaders to efficiently mobilize both online and in the physical world
- They can connect to an international audience—outreach strategy is more important than political borders
- And one Big Risk—where social media users are a small fraction of the overall population, important to be aware that the online population and discourse might not be representative of the real thing

References

1. ComScore report FIF—India Digital-Future In Focus—Author in possession of the report
2. http://www.coolage.in/2013/07/19/use-emerging-technologies-social-media-for-development-sam-pi/
3. http://esummit2012.se/files/download/255/iusxrdon
4. (http://www.newsday.com/opinion/oped/wadhwa-how-social-media-changed-the-world-1.6962077)
5. http://www.hindustantimes.com/technology/apps-updates/microsoft-launches-new-app-for-women-s-safety/article1-1166528.aspx
6. http://forbesindia.com/blog/technology/governments-love-hate-relationship-with-social-media/
7. http://thesocialmediamonthly.com/how-social-media-has-changed-politics-its-not-just-tactics/
8. http://www.politico.com/news/stories/0311/51 457.html
9. Socially Elected / Why Social Media Wins Campaigns Page 11 / Craig Agranoff and Herbert Tabin

10. http://ibnlive.in.com/news/aap-follows-obamas-campaign-strategy-for-delhi-polls/432316-80-258.html

11. http://www.pbs.org/newshour/bb/media/july-dec12/download_11-16.html

12. http://timesofindia.indiatimes.com/home/specials/assembly-elections-2013/madhya-pradesh-assembly-elections/Modi-Run-Shivraj-App-violate-election-code-Congress/articleshow/24437967.cms

13. http://www.iamai.in/PRelease_detail.aspx?nid=31901&NMonth=10&NYear=2013

14. http://www.iamai.in/PRelease_detail.aspx?nid=3222&NMonth=11&NYear=2013

15. http://www.hindustantimes.com/specials/coverage/myindia-myvote/chunk-ht-ui-myindiamyvote-leadingstories/will-young-indians-vote/sp-article10-1146304.aspx

16. http://indiatoday.intoday.in/story/shashi-tharoor-blog-india67-india-today-independence-special/1/298680.html

17. http://thesocialmediamonthly.com/how-social-media-has-changed-politics-its-not-just-tactics/

3

Social Media and Demographics

Winning this youth vote bank is critical for a party that wants to form the government. With more than 50 percent of India's population below the age of 25, one will not be wrong to assume that these new voters are technology-friendly. Add to this the number of social media users in urban India that reached 78 million by June 2013, according to a report by IAMAI and IMRB International, and this number is expected to multiply through 2014. All this growth comes on the back of rising Internet penetration due to increasing affordability of smartphones and availability of cost-effective data plans. The survey was conducted across 35 cities of the country. The report said social networking through mobile phones is widely observed with 19.8 million users accessing websites on mobiles.

There is no doubt at the moment that Facebook is the leading website accessed by 96 percent of all social media users and it is most used to connect with friends, publishing content, and searching contacts. Mostly all phones come with a Facebook app and the latter has also become a trigger for phone sales.

Once the data is spliced, the report shows how 'non-working women' are tipped to be the next emerging demographic segment with nearly 10 percent of them accessing social media. They have access to online stores, communities, common interests, and are actively participating in building opinion.

It also highlighted that networking sites are increasingly used by political institutions and 2–5 percent of election budgets are estimated to be spent on social media initiatives. 'Small-scale campaign responsibilities are usually outsourced by the political parties whereas critical election campaigns are managed in-house by the party experts,' it says. The report estimates that investing in various social media initiatives could lead to a vote swing of around 3–4 percent among the users in the country. Given the sheer size of the active online community, it is hard to predict the political preference of this emerging group. However, observers say the impact of social media on election outcome wouldn't be substantial in the near future.

YOUNG OR OLD?

Younger men and women, aged between 35–44 years have emerged as power users according to ComScore's report on India Digital: Future In Focus. 'Three-quarters of India's Online populations under 35. Males in the segment and women aged 35–44 are amongst the heaviest users.' Facebook leads the charge there with a 28 percent jump in users of the social networking site in the last twelve months.

Statistics shared by the ComScore report suggest that social media is no longer just for the new kid on the block. Social media goes beyond the young and the infatuated bunch. It's serious business with serious players. So from sit-at-home moms, grandparents, restless youth, opinionated neighbours, and leaders in any and every field—they are all on social media. They are all engaging. They are all adding to the network. They are all also *influencing*. Influence is that delicate hypothesis which multiplies, predicts, and defines the behaviour in the social network and online connections.

In addition to influence, social media in the digital world has become the new form of 'empowerment'. Be it politics or pure consumption of goods, the consumer or voter feels their say is crucial. Santosh Desai who has worked on brand strategy in corporate India says, 'Digital is democratic, collaborative, connected and simultaneous. Brands of the future will have to accept the fact that the power to influence a consumer has shifted from brand managers to brand users. The centralized grip of power structures that made brands have a guarded conversation with the user needs to be decentralized. Brands need to take cognizance that consumers today have their own say and they will listen to only what they want to listen and not what brands want them to listen.'[1]

Hence, brands—both business and political—need platform-focused social media strategies in the digital world, rather than a diluted strategy that aims to be everywhere at once. They need to track, influence, and then select the appropriate medium and approach. What matters is behaviour and demographics. The rise of social media comes at a time when information consumption patterns are changing. Behaviour of individuals as a 'social being' is driven by what others are doing. Social media is central to the capturing of this. There are instant reactions, allowing for co-participation and that's the bedrock of social media. From a strategic point of view, political campaigns now use social media to sow an idea and then allow it to multiply through online communities of its fans, followers, and friends. It is instant and campaigns, conversations, and ideas just multiply fast and the reach can be unlimited if it is good. Campaign strategists have realized the power of sharing and this election will definitely be the first big experiment with social media.

CONSUMPTION OF MEDIA AND MAKING CHOICES

What lies at the heart of this confluence of social media, demographics, and choice decisions is how we consume anything that is available online. Consumption today is driven by choices made online which are further decided by predictive algorithms and analysis. Here, consumption is loosely defined as absorption of ideas, product purchases, opinion triggers, and more. The advertising we see on Google or on our Facebook page is led by our past searches on Google, or our likes on Facebook. Data giants claim that they are in the business of organizing chaos into information, and information into value—that assumption by its very logic is going to break the population into silos and packets. The deeper question then is: Is social media revolution restricting our choices or letting us become more open minded and explore new things and ideas? If we are going to be tracked based on predictive and previous selections, isn't the networking media making us narrow in our choices? Are we giving up the idea of exploring the new because only certain posts are visible to us? Well-known academic Professor Mathew Baum at the Harvard Kennedy School describes it as 'self-segregated information streams' which reinforce people's existing beliefs instead of challenging them. Where consumers keep returning to sources that cater to their political or social leanings and not new ones—'a fractured media marketplace.' Does it in some way imply that content can be controlled by those with resources? Can owners of technology and power sway opinion far more than those who are digitally deprived? This can be dangerous as it limits the scope for consensus, debate, and tolerance of listening to the opposing views. In some ways, the media coverage of US elections was a good reflection of such reinforcement of beliefs where Republicans largely got their news from Fox News which led them to further believe in what they already wanted to hear. Extreme polarization leads to a further gap between opposing views which may be one of the most undesirable outcomes of social media excesses.

If you like the Narendra Modi fan page, your friends and family will be made aware of your liking and that in a way is a method to influence them. The post on your timeline creates a news feed that your friends are seeing allowing peer influence. On the other hand that one 'like' allows other pages linked to Modi, Gujarat, BJP to then show up on your sponsored posts list to encourage you to like those too. Whether or not you are a right-winger, you have got slotted somewhere in a formula in the world wide social network. The complex questions about the rules that will protect privacy for individuals on one hand and free information flows on the other are yet to be answered. And this is despite the security and privacy settings. Social network algorithms slot every individual even though they may not be strictly deserving of the same. You may be curious about a party's politics but that doesn't make you a part of them. Networking sites are yet to find qualitative answers to making choices. On one hand we self-filter by selecting what to follow and what not to and therefore turn the conversation in the direction we desire to. At the same time, we become susceptible of only getting to hear what we want to.

This takes us to the next question—does social media also, to borrow a phrase from Noam Chomsky, manufacture consent? Does it have plenty of sway? According to well-known brand guru Harish Bijoor, 'Yes it does. It is also incidentally a medium where opinion leaders hold plenty of sway. Look at any terrain; whether it be politics, banking, consumer marketing, FMCG, durables, there are opinon leaders who have a following they leverage. To an extent these opinion leaders pre-digest the subject and make it friendly enough for all to have a say in it. To that extent, social media is not really as social as it seems.' The common person on social media is bombarded with information and ideas, many of which are hard to break down and digitally digest. Meena Yadav is a conscious citizen engaged with the civil society. She finds social media a great outlet to vent and share discontentment with political parties. However, she is convinced that social media too is a victim of manufacturing 'consent.'

'It does concern me. Many a time the media gives a distorted view. It's hard to imagine every form of media is spared from being corrupt because there are different factors that drive the media too.'

A study done in the United States in 2010 surveyed over 60 million Facebook messages on a political issue. The results showed that the FB messages shared by political organizations with potential voters, 'directly influenced political self-expression, information–seeking and real world voting behaviour of millions of people. Furthermore, the messages not only influenced the users who received them but also the user's friends and friends of friends.'[2] The paper concluded that the effectiveness of these messages increased where people knew each other face to face and that strong ties between people are a prerequisite to spreading certain kinds of behaviours both online and in the real world. So can friends influence who you vote for? And is that a game-changing concept? The paper explains that voter mobilization experiments of contacting potential voters have had a small effect on turnouts but adds that 'small' is a relative concept. It says, 'The ability to reach large populations online means that even small effect could yield behaviour changes for millions of people.'

In the book, *I'll Have What She's Having: Mapping Social Behavior*, Mark Earls and his co-authors examine the processes by which ideas spread through our social networks. Neal Cole's review of the book articulates some important points in the GreenBookBlog.[3] Are people even aware there is inadvertent imitation of thoughts and ideas on the social network? 'The book explains there are numerous reasons why we imitate other people, but essentially herd behaviour is at the heart of the dispersion of ideas, behavioural change and innovation through our social networks.' The authors use the analogy of forest fires to study mass behaviour. It infers that forest fires that spread do not concern themselves with the characteristics of an individual tree and what it is made of. Instead they treat each tree as flammable material in a grid system. What matters is how close trees are to other trees and how they interact with each other.'

The book suggests that social learning by a few gets amplified as copying by the masses. It describes how ideas, behaviour, and culture spread through the simple means of doing what others do.

VOTING BEHAVIOUR

In the last couple of decades, voting turnouts have been poor in India. But the recent upsurge in social consciousness has forced many to come out and walk the talk. Between 1984 and 2009, parliamentary election turnout swung between a low of 56 percent in 1991 to a maximum high of 64 percent in 1984. This time in 2013 during the state elections—Delhi, for example—the turnout was record breaking, at nearly 67 percent.[4] Some of this has to do with voters unshackling themselves from being armchair opinion makers to actual voters. The anti- incumbency within the urban voter, the impatience with corruption, and the general sense of gloom did push people out of their homes but to what extent is very difficult to ascertain. What can be somewhat understood is how social media has influenced their voting behaviour. A study conducted by Shoeb Ahmed Khan in first half of 2013 shows how different media impacts the voting behaviour in people and attempts to gather insights on what leads them into that decision. Social media may not top the 'influencer' chart but it's very much central to it. The survey clearly shows that, despite being outranked by traditional forms of media, content on social media does impact voting decisions in some way or the other.

So here's what the ranking looks like in terms of what media changes voting behaviour.[5]

1. Television, newspapers, and magazines
2. Radio
3. News websites
4. Facebook
5. Twitter

6. Blogs
7. Forums and boards
8. Official websites

The paper further goes on to conclude that online chatter by the general public on platforms like Twitter, Facebook, and Forums has an influence on an individual's political opinion more than content shared by official accounts of political parties and politicians. The research revealed that even though the public does not trust official channels of communication, they would still like to be able to find their local politician on social media to be able to voice their issues and make themselves heard. Brand experts believe it makes sense for politicians and parties to address citizens' queries on a variety of social, municipal, and national matters and engage with them. It is hence an important medium of propagating your mandate to the general public and assuring your voter that you have an ear for their problems.

WHICH IDEOLOGY HAS THE 'SOCIAL' ADVANTAGE?

Social media promises to be an important link to politics for now. The country has seen in the last decade, a general surge in political opinion, where in the youth of the country are participative in political discourse or hold political affilia-tions. Unlike many other countries, in India young people are not averse to openly discussing politics or sharing their opinions on political matters. A study done by Pew Research quoted by BBC suggests that nearly 45 percent of Indian web users connect on social media to discuss politics.[6] This is a good indication as to why Indian politicians are rushing to get on board, set up Facebook pages, Twitter handles, and communicating directly with their vote bank online. It is clear that those who can transform their top-down style of talking to voters to a way of engaging with them in a more one on one, level playing way, they are bound to be the winners. For the citizens, social media presence of politicians is almost like a direct hotline with them. Gimmicks by the smart politicians today include replying back once in a while to an ordinary citizen thus winning loyalty forever and coming across as humble and considerate.

Harish Bijoor feels that being on social media for politicians is no longer a choice. He says, 'The point of social media is that you must be on it. You must be on it not only to make your brand, but to stop anyone from breaking your brand. Social media may not make brands for some, but it can surely break brands. When politicians ask me if they should be on social media, I tell them, you must, must be. Either get social, or be anti-social!' Suddenly there is the idea of a 'political brand' being talked about. Leaders want to understand their mileage and use media and networking sites to position themselves. There is a desire to appeal to the youth. Brand expert Lloyd Mathias of Green Bean Ventures shares that social media is intrinsically linked with sharping a brand. 'It has ensured a strong resonance with the youth.'

Given that the medium is fast, viral, and widespread, does it reward the first movers? Does the one who connects first with the desired demographic group have the advantage? Narendra Modi's connect with the youth through all available social media platforms is clearly in stark contrast to the Congress front runner for the PM who refuses to even get online to communicate with the youth. Another good example is that of the Aam Aadmi Party which too has clearly established that when you lack the big bucks, social media can be the gamechanger in communicating to those who support you. It has also helped to discover new voters who until now were isolated from the direct reach. The role of networking sites on politics is well established by the fact that the Election Commission of India has worked on rules and regulations to monitor use of posts, tweets etc. during election campaigning.

Social media makes it possible, it transcends the physical boundaries, and brings together the demographic, consumption behaviour and political choice making at the fingertips of the campaign manager. It has added an element of engagement, of public response and of scrutiny, making 'social' sanction very important for politicians. Before social media came around, the talk was in people's drawing rooms. Those who saw it on television would have had their personal opinions and may have shared them with friends and family, but social media has turned everything into a rallying point. The social media push helps politicians to not only address new and potential voters but also to use existing mass of support to further their cause by becoming voluntary nodes of the campaign. Today, social media has given mainstream media a run for its money, where the latter is picking up news, sound bites (in tweets, YouTube clips, posts) from the former. Social media's power over the elections comes in highlighting sentiment, breaking the comfort zone, taking on ideologies head on, and sway thinking in their favour. No politician can underestimate the power of social media today.

REFERENCES

1. [http://santoshdesai.com/2012/04/india-social-summit-2012-3/]
2. http://fowler.ucsd.edu/massive_turnout.pdf
3. http://www.greenbookblog.org/2012/10/31/social-networks-human-behavior/
4. http://www.idea.int/vt/countryview.cfm?CountryCode=IN
5. Impact of social media on voting behavior. White Paper 24/5/2013 by Shoeb Ahmed Khan, Intern-MSL India
6. http://www.bbc.co.uk/news/business-21831185

4

Selecting the Right Tools for
Social Media

What role does social media play in an election campaign? Do election volunteers and social media teams know what's needed to be a winner in today's election scene? Are Indian political parties willing to change, adapt, rewind and plan forward with respect to media platforms? What kind of media can generate the optimum political returns? To borrow from economics, it would be fair to say that social media is a necessary condition for political campaigning but not a sufficient one. As an aid for elections, politicians have turned a keen eye to learn and use social media. As several examples in the US, UK, and now even India have shown, whatever the election outcome, Twitter and Facebook will come up as winners as they remain an active medium for communication and campaigning. Political debates have moved from just being part of television sets to include the online world. While you cannot just be on social media and must have all offline channels open for information sharing and engagement, it's worth looking at the options before politicians and their teams in the election season. 'Social media is creating new brands.

As a politician, being on it is important by way of building your political brand' says film maker Shekhar Kapur who runs a social media platform to crowdsource creative content and recently anchored a political show Pradhan Mantri. 'It is the idea of influence that is changing things as influence is all that matters in today's networked world.'

TWITTER

The hashtag is the latest weapon in Indian politics. For those who have been on Twitter from the start and those who are learning to squeeze speeches into 140 characters, the blue birdie has created a hornet's nest in every party's communication strategy. Twitter serves different purposes for different people—a newsfeed, a social media ticker, a political megaphone, or a message medium. For campaigns and elected officials, it is a way to connect directly with constituents and other interested observers, circumventing traditional media. For debates, it's the instrument to set the stage and sow the idea in the minds of the public. For people, it's a great platform to voice opinions and critique flexibly. Staying off Twitter means being on the outside of some of the most engaging political discourses involving political supporters, campaign strategists, other politicians, and journalists. 'Twitter is clearly the better media because it enables quick articulation and communication to a wide audience,' expresses Ganesh Natarajan, Chairman of Nasscom and global CEO of Zensar who is among the few Indian executives active on Twitter. About 10,000 tweets do the rounds every second. Twitter also echoes people's choices and views. It brings them together. It's allows them to get behind issues they are passionate about; the downside of this are trolls, who find power in numbers too. Twitter feed is a great on-spot meter of moods, ideas, reactions, and behaviours.

Practically all leaders of state are on Twitter, from Presidents to Prime Ministers, to popular leaders in film, culture, and sports. They have big followings. Barack Obama tops the political charts with about 36 million followers during American elections, the Turkish PM with over 3 million followers, late Hugo Chavez with over 4 million, India's Narendra Modi with about 3 million, and Indian Prime Minister's office with just under a million. The watershed in social media use in elections was the 2008 election. According to one estimate, there are now more tweets sent every two days than had ever been sent prior to the 2008 American election. This increased popularity of the social network and the impact of Twitter in the following elections of 2012 as well in the United States.[1]

The world's top leaders have used this social media to declare various 'events'. In 2008, Barack Obama made his victory announcement on Twitter. Mitt Romney announced his plan to run for President in the 2012 campaign via a tweet. In India, too, it's a tool that most public figures in general, and politicians in particular have come to use. It is not only a medium for denizens to communicate with world leaders but also a way for these leaders to communicate with each other. On the one hand, it's a broadcast tool and on the other, it allows access and engagement. The Prime Minister's office in India uses its @PMOIndia handle effectively to make announcements or send out instant reactions—where it wants to—on key issues.

Gujarat's Chief Minister Narendra Modi became a pied piper on Twitterverse, catapulting his controversial popularity to something substantial as he engaged with his online audience. It's a matter of debate whether his right wing strong views are appropriate or not but what he has managed to do is get India's saffron brigade on to Twitter and channeled them into an army of volunteer-workers on social media.

Leaders also grab social media headlines. Sushma Swaraj, senior leader of the BJP, used Twitter to express a rather controversial view about ruling party Congress. On 27 October, 2013, Swaraj tweeted that the Congress party's General Secretary Digvijay Singh was better than the party's Vice President Rahul Gandhi. 'Even I think Digvijay Singh ji is a better candidate than Rahul Gandhi. @digvijaya_28.' This was retweeted nearly 1000 times.

Also in October 2013, Congress declared it would start live-tweeting party Vice President Rahul Gandhi's speeches. A digital team accompanies Rahul Gandhi to areas he goes for rallies. The Aam Aadmi Party effectively used Twitter to do fact–checks, amplify their message by raising questions, and gaining quick insights into the mood of people over key issues and often against the ruling government. These included controversial matters like RTI, CWG, and other cases.

Politicians 'really don't have a choice, they have to engage on Twitter,' said Marcus Messner, a professor at the School of Mass Communications at Virginia Commonwealth University.[2] Some are actively using it to give statements, tweeting rallies, while others to stir a controversy. By all means, it's the simplest and fastest tool to reach people.

It's also a personality tool for politicians. It's an image-building piece of their career. It allows people to show off their good work as well and create a hero-like digital aura. Compared with other social media, Twitter remains the least tedious because it's driven by just 140 characters, and can be effective without picture posts as is the case of other social sites, making it a good reason why so many world leaders have latched on to it. Twitter user interface could hardly be simpler as a quick glance gives you enough information. For instant politics and news, Facebook is increasingly cluttered with a myriad of applications, information feeds, photos, ads, etc. The Twiplomacy study for 2013 found that more than three-quarters (77.7 percent) of world leaders have a Twitter account. Presidents, prime ministers, foreign ministers or their respective administrations in 153 countries have a presence on Twitter. The website shares that the Indian Prime Minister is quite active with an average of almost 5 tweets a day. It also highlights PMO's most shared tweet was the one put out after the Delhi gang-rape case in December 2012. 'While she may have lost her battle for life, it is up to us all to ensure that her death will not have been in vain.'[3]

Twitter's popularity also has to do with how simple it is to get on to it, and get tweeting. 'For anyone who needs to build a personal brand, be it a writer, a celebrity, or a company's CEO, the Twitter learning curve is shorter. You tweet, people follow, and your network grows,' says Alyson Shontell in a piece for the *Business Insider*.[4] The example of Aam Aadmi Party is very relevant to this 'short learning curve.' Since its inception in November 2012, the party took to social media in a big way but also used Twitter most effectively in its favour. It was able to garner around 2,50,000 followers in a short time. Importantly, during its very first election as a fledging party in December 2013, AAP was leading on Twitter—it was almost as if it was 'polled in' on the social media space. 'Twitter was much more effective when it came to making news in media,' says Ankit Lal, head of IT and social media at AAP. Twitter is also the space where the party got accolades from the Twitterati, instantly validating AAP's existence and its struggle to make its presence felt in a 60-year-old BJP-Congress party system.

So it's this spontaneity about Twitter, these instant reactions that make it more exciting than other social media platforms, particularly to politicians, journalists, and those 'wired' in. Some believe it's the new news channel. Kapur believes it is now 'the biggest News Channel in the world...'

'What is astonishing about Twitter is that in the seven years since it was founded as a side project to share messages among a group of friends, it has become the de facto newswire for the planet,' says John Naughton in *The Observer*.[5] Britain's David Cameron was among those who were cautious about what he called the 'instantness' and early use of Twitter as a political tool, famously telling a radio show in 2009, when he was leader of the opposition, that 'too many tweets might make a twat.'[6] His views may have altered somewhat now as he is on Twitter.

There is no doubt that journalists today get a lot of their political headlines from Twitter. More so if they are laced with sarcasm, aim snipes at other leaders, or are entirely politically incorrect. Admits PR professional Soni Mahdi Aggarwal, 'While Twitter offers direct communication and spontaneity, it can however get the politician into trouble sometimes.' Mega scandals have been triggered by eyebrow-raising tweets. There are many instances of this. In the United States former Congressman Anthony Weiner made global headlines. The New York Democrat's sexting scandal came to light after he accidentally posted a lewd photograph of his crotch on Twitter. He later tried to extricate himself of the situation with a slipshod cover-up, and eventually admitted to a mistake. India has had its own share of Twitter faux pas. BJP's prime ministerial candidate Narendra Modi became a laughing stock on social networking site Twitter for inadvertently spelling 'Lotus' (the election symbol of BJP) as 'Louts' (awkward brutish person).[7]

Rahul Gandhi has often been criticized for staying away from Twitter and social media but still makes headlines on social media. Rahul Gandhi's 'escape velocity' metaphor on Dalit empowerment in a speech may be one of the most joked-about comments on Twitter in 2013. He used astronomy to criticize Mayawati's pro-Dalit party Bahujan Samaj Party, saying she had done little to lift them in society. 'A Dalit needs the escape velocity of Jupiter to achieve success,' Rahul Gandhi commented, spurring the Twitter world to break into witty and some insulting references to 'escape velocity.' One @shikha_shrivas tweeted, 'The 2013 Nobel prize in Physics is about to be announced. #Escapevelocity. Hmm was he bidding for that?' And then there was @siddharth426 who said, 'Talking about Dalits using terms of Physics. It's like Sunny Leone giving a lecture on governing economics. #Pappu'.

Despite the good, the bad, and the ugly of Twitter, here is a tool that permits them all to create and promote hashtags that can popularize a certain philosophy and campaign. Social media teams have the option of making a strategy in a way that hashtags become as good as keywords and throw up the impulses of any campaign in search engines. Additionally, campaign research can get a boost with a tweet-stick test (as opposed to a dipstick check!). It's a quick barometer to any question posed and provides a big picture view of the mood and sentiment. Saritha Rai, in a special column for *Forbes*, asserts that the digital face-off between political parties and their leaders has already reached a shrill extreme even before electioneering has begun. 'The main Congress and BJP set up what are dubbed "digital war rooms" and mandated that leaders get active on Twitter. Each party is mobilizing thousands of impassioned supporters on social networks,' she explains.[8] Twitter has the ability to instantly rile up people and to help garner online support. Therefore, strategies to engage with the medium must be closely followed and thought out.

Given that social media brings people face to face with their leaders, it's imperative that politicians are cognizant of this as a marketing tool and extract mileage of the same. As Seth Godin once said, 'Marketing is no longer about the stuff that you make, but about the stories you tell.' For politicians social media platforms are perfect for telling stories. Sharing experiences. Twitter, in that sense, is an extension of them. It's not just someone else's responsibility because it bears their stamp on it. For politicians still wondering how to craft a strategy, they must ensure they personalize their accounts and stay up to date with what is being tweeted on their behalf by their team. Barack Obama used and publicized his style. He tweeted as well and made it clear when a tweet ended with '-BO', it was him and not his campaign manager tweeting. Perhaps Obama's approach could inspire Indian leaders too? AAP leader Arvind Kejriwal's team says he tweets entirely on his own and doesn't let anyone else take charge of his handle. One can say the same about BJD MP Jay Panda, of Congress's Shashi Tharoor. In case of Narendra Modi, he has a team to tweet on his behalf but no tweet is put out without his tacit approval say his party strategists. There is no evidence to suggest the Indian PM has ever tweeted himself, although he is aware of how social media works. Pankaj Pachauri, the media advisor to the Prime Minister says, 'We have explained the concept to him. We do a quarterly feedback with him on all such social media activities.'

Twiplomacy study shows that almost half of the accounts of political leaders featured are personal accounts. '90 heads of state, 61 heads of government and 53 foreign ministers have personal accounts on Twitter and a third of these do tweet themselves, but only 14 tweet on a regular basis.'[9]

As a political tool, Twitter is about connecting with people and generating conversations about topics. Hashtags play a big role here. Twitter turned the use of hashtags into an idea of its own. So today hashtags act as hyperlinks and let you launch search queries of that keyword. This is the ultimate goal of any campaign manager—creating a search tag that is pumped up by his team, followers of his ideas, and then made to 'trend.'

On Twitter, trending topics help users discover the hottest emerging topics people are talking about as they break, rather than the total volume of conversation about a topic, making the platform a great place to keep up with the latest events and news. In its list of what captured the country's attention for much of 2013, in politics, Modi was the top trended tag[10] followed by Rahul Gandhi, BJP, Nitish Kumar, DelhiWantsAAP, Pawan Bansal, Chintan Shivir, Saheb, Pak PM, and DMK.

Twitter has somewhat come full circle in India. From being feared and avoided, it is now being embraced by leaders. In that sense, Union Minister Shashi Tharoor had the last laugh on this one. In a recent article, he pointed out how politicians have suddenly realized the potential of this medium when four years ago he was being criticized for being online. 'When I started with Twitter four years ago, everyone was critical of me as being in the political space it was not a serious thing for a politician to do.'

WHY TWITTER MATTERS

- ✤ Short, snappy, and quick: It's short, formal, and lends itself to share information quickly, making it impersonal and effective. It also focuses on one thought given its restricted 140-characters

- ✤ Immediate: The micro-blogging site allows for real-time communication. Twitter is compared to Facebook and other social platforms, including blogs. It is more headline centric and does not depend on greater detailing and views

- ✤ Connects one on one: It's a one on one medium. Leaders and people can reach out to each other directly over debates, information exchange, or through built-in basics like sharing, retweeting, or replying to a tweet.

- ✤ Real-time reaction: During Rahul Gandhi's speeches or Narendra Modi's rallies, voters and potential supporters are able to react to their discourse. Tweeple can comment to seek the reaction of others by retweeing or with mentions. In the American context, even today, Barack Obama's image of hugging his wife Michelle right after the re-election of 2012, remains the most retweeted photo and his victory tweet the most retweeted. One estimate suggests that when news of Obama's re-election broke, there were 3,27,452 related tweets posted every minute

- ✤ Trends: Twitter is a perfect barometer to gauge what's trending at that moment within the audience and public at large. As the site's algorithm throws up the trending subjects that are dominating conversation, it's a great space to know what's occupying the mind of voters and supporters

- Social media amplifier: The book *Socially Elected* by Craig Agranoff and Herbert Tabin states, 'Think of Twitter as your campaign's megaphone or the digital equivalent of letter writing campaigns and protest groups chanting your campaign.' In India, in the case of the Anna Hazare movement—the India Against Corruption campaign, the tool was primarily used to mobilize people. During the Delhi gang-rape case, it was used to share details of night vigils, candle light marches, and so on

- Live debates and conferences: Twitter chats, conferences and discussions have become a great way of reaching a lot of people by hosting on Twitter. The attendance is instant, the infrastructure is just the smartphone and so there is no need for elaborate arrangements or planning. A politician or a campaigner can instantly call for a discussion or debate on a burning issue and get the conversation going. This also means that with social media around, one doesn't have to wait to watch TV alone to get a debate in play. The idea of prime time is almost all the time on social media

- Inexpensive: Thanks to social media, political campaigns can now send out messages quickly, without relying on expensive TV ads and time-consuming press interviews. Aam Aadmi Party used it because they were strapped for funds to use any other mass media to call for protests at Jantar Mantar, a monument in Delhi, which became symbolic for aggregation of crowds against the government. It works both ways—as an information disseminator and also lends a voice to people who have not had one. For voters, social media has redefined transparency in politics.

In United States and more recently in the State elections in Delhi, it gave citizens an opportunity to let their voices be heard

FACEBOOK

Facebook is the one platform that has almost everyone in its fold from young to old, thought leaders, opinion makers and more. According to ComScore, in 2012, Facebook.com had a reach of 83.4 percent in India, meaning around 4 out of 5 online Indians visited the popular social networking site. Little wonder then that it is a power instrument for those wanting to influence opinion. Facebook by itself has launched several political tools within its perimeter to get leaders to engage with people on board. Facebook is clearly not just about 'checking in' or posting your dog's cutest video. Its power and reach make it a most effective space to lock attention of constituents that matter to organizations and people. Additionally, plugins now allow people to just about participate and 'like' anything on any website if you are logged into your account. It's a great reflection of demographics as it is of using data analytics to your favour. It's no surprise that the number of 'likes' for a political campaign, party fan page, or leader's profile has become a sort of a de facto popularity metre. 'It has become the centrestage for votes to not only broadcast political affiliations but also brag about electoral activities,' the authors explain in the book *Socially Elected*.[11]

So clearly, the view of cyber world is important. Some analysis can be done on the popularity charts of politicians by analysing the likes or followers and 'how many were talking about it'—a parameter that defines engagement levels for every Facebook post. Just before this book went into publication, the Facebook page of Narendra Modi was not only verified and had 7.1 million likes, there were 8,45,782 people talking about the page. In Congress, Sonia Gandhi and Rahul Gandhi's individual pages were neither verified nor active with likes of between 70,000 and 26,000 respectively. Aam Aadmi Party, with its verified account, had over 7,00,000 likes with a third of its fans talking about it.

Facebook verifies pages of important figures by contacting them and making sure that they are not imposters operating it. For other politicians, a website called videathink.com did a piece around UP elections in the year 2012 measuring Facebook interactivity of some politicians. Arunima Rai of videathink.com shared in an article, 'Akhilesh Yadav's official Facebook page is nothing more than a marketing gimmick. It was extremely active before 2012 legislative assembly elections of Uttar Pradesh. After thumping victory of SP in the 2012 election, the Akhilesh Yadav official FB page is inactive in comparison of activity before 2012 election.'[12]

Facebook's own prescription for political campaigns include some great but basic ideas. User engagement remains a priority. 'Create an interactive experience by involving your audience in the discussion. Gauging the opinions of your constituents using Facebook Questions or encouraging fans of your Page to submit questions or comments creates a genuine dialogue between politicians and their supporters,' the prescription piece advises.[13]

If engagement is top priority, then the Facebook fan page must lead people somewhere for them to generate appropriate results for the campaign's goal. In that sense, Facebook and the party's website must feed into each other and play to their strengths. 'Facebook is more of a reflection and sharing medium while Twitter can spread messages and themes like wildfire,' shares Ganesh Natrajan who also works for India's tech-telecom body Nasscom besides being the CEO of Zensar Tech. For example, AAP managed to use a lot of their social media posts to eventually drive people to the AAP website where they sought donations. On Narendra Modi's Facebook page, you'd often find posts with links that open up the website's video or audio streaming for his fans. Crosslinking materials and feeding the website to Facebook and Facebook to the website are critical to the 'network' of being social.

What's helped on this front is Facebook introducing hashtags, as well. The more descriptive, perhaps lengthy, posts along with the hashtags at the end or as a footnote allows for unobtrusive reading unlike Twitter, where hashtags consume precious characters. On a Facebook wall post, you can address hashtags after a long paragraph by giving a few sentence breaks. What this did for politics and Facebook is that it allowed for more people to engage in discussions that were otherwise just restricted to friends or friends of friends. Now even strangers may find public posts based on hashtag searches. Additionally, taking note of the how quickly the 'trending' feature of twitter was absorbed by news, media organisations and users across the world, Facebook introduced the trending and follow features. Now people can follow others even if they can't be friends. This feature has worked well for leaders and other political fan pages. The trending feature picks on what's most talked about among its 1.2 billion users to suggest topics of choice.

Despite appropriate strategies and campaign management, there is always the risk of misuse and Facebook abuse, especially towards leaders in a hurry. The social media wildfire is so strong that it has led many to believe they could take shortcuts to garner popoularity. On Facebook, for example, there are now umpteen websites advertising instant 'likes' in exchange for money. In early 2013, Indian politician Ashok Gehlot from Rajasthan was criticized for allegedly 'buying' likes from Turkey as his fan page showed a disproportionate increase in the number of likes. This forced BJP, other right-wing sites to mock him saying, 'Seems Gehlot is more popular in Istanbul than he is in Jaipur.'[14]. Such reports also surfaced for some other Congress politicians like Ajay Maken and General Secretary Digvijaya Singh. Majority of their fans—even more than those from India—came from Turkey. What is evident is that the web is infiltrated with social media sites offering to use algorithms to notch up your fanbase. An undercover operation by Cobrapost in November 2013 exposed how IT companies in India may have been using social media platforms such as Facebook, Twitter, and YouTube to help politicians artificially boost their popularity. In a sting operation named 'Operation Blue Virus', the web portal, Cobrapost alleged that IT companies offered their clients the option to indulge in negative publicity against a political leader or a party, or a corporate house, at the behest of their opposite camp, for money.[15] In the end, these fake likes are going be useless since those aren't the fans that will 'engage' and generate opinions. Any effort to increase you fan base will be futile as the purpose of social media is to ensure it remains participative. Showing off fans can only be a temporary exercise that's bound to fail you in the long term.

Facebook warns users on its website FAQs, 'Certain websites promise to provide large numbers of likes for your Page if you sign up and give them money. These websites typically use deceptive practices or are scams. People who like your Page this way will be less valuable to your Page because they won't necessarily have a genuine interest in what your Page is about.'

FACEBOOK'S POLITICAL PRESCRIPTION FOR POSTS

- ✤ Try to upload an image or photo with every post. We find that posts with images get twice the amount of engagement as compared to other posts
- ✤ Schedule posts between 9 and 10 pm. We've found this hour is one of the most engaging on Facebook
- ✤ Post at least once every day. It keeps your supporters more engaged and keeps your content in their news feeds
- ✤ Use Facebook ads to promote your content, gain new fans, and increase engagement
- ✤ Create an interactive experience by involving your audience in the discussion. Gauging the opinions of your constituents using Facebook Questions or encouraging fans of your Page to submit questions or comments, creates a genuine dialogue between politicians and their supporters
- ✤ Post in your own voice. Facebook users have come to expect a genuine experience when engaging with the friends and causes they value the most
- ✤ Go multimedia! Including live or pre-recorded video segments on your Page is a great way to involve supporters in the goings-on of your campaign

So is there any discourse on which is better for politics —Twitter or facebook? Ankit Lal, the head of IT and social media at the Aam Aadmi Party says both were equally important, 'but had different utilities. In the initial days FB was better utilized as we were bit weak on Twitter but then we pulled up and towards the end both performed equally well.'

LINKEDIN

Most politicians overlook using Linkedin in a bid to accumulate likes, shares, and followers. Unlike Facebook and Twitter, this platform doesn't necessarily offer direct, megaphone capabilities, but that's doesn't mean it's not powerful or useful. It remains an under-utilized space for political campaigning. Even though it is actually one of the older players in this space, it's typically meant for professionals to connect with each other or for job opportunities. For political leaders, a Linkedin account only rounds up the social media image and beliefs the individual is trying to project, just like it does for a small business owner or an executive in transition.

Otherwise designed to be a business tool, Neal Schaffer, the Editor of Maximise Social Business Dot Com, picks three reasons for not ignoring Linkedin.[16]

Brand your profile

It should stand what you stand for and should advertise your platform, assuming you have one. Why beat around the bush when you can directly communicate with almost 40 million professionals?

Join groups that you want to be aligned with

If, for instance, there is a solar energy group and that is what you are campaigning for, why not join this type of group and contribute? In fact, you can have your political staff trolling the Discussion Boards and News Articles looking for new ideas and generating opinions that may help further enhance your political views.

Connect and make allies

As in real life, networking is important in politics. If you are in a particular position in government, isn't there a natural affinity to be connected and exchange best practices with similar public officers throughout the country if not the world? Furthermore, there is always necessary collaboration between the public office and businesses and education, so why not utilize Linkedin to create a virtual network of potential people that could be major allies in your future?

There are global leaders who have embraced Linkedin. One of them is British Prime Minister David Cameron. BBC quoted Downing Street in an article to suggest Cameron's aim is 'to connect in the online places where business connects', with virtual friendships being made 'to reflect the people and businesses the Prime Minister comes into contact within the course of his duties'.[17] If one was to put an image beside the definition of a 'business' Prime Minister, it would be Cameron's, who has doggedly pushed for business collaborations between the UK and other countries. Perhaps this intent of his got him first moving on Linkedin with a view to keep a finger on the pulse of global businesses and people associated with it. In India, few leaders have embraced it. Narendra Modi has over 500 connections with an account managed by BJP Samvad Cell.[18] Bill Gates, Richard Branson, and Barack Obama are on Linkedin's Influencer platform. Within 48 hours, Bill Gates' first Influencer post on Linkedin generated more than 1 million page views.

In Asia, there are several leaders who have recently come on board the Influencer platform, such as Mike Smith (CEO of ANZ Banking Group), Tony Fernandes (Group CEO, AirAsia), and Shinzo Abe (Prime Minister of Japan). In India, just over the last few months, Linkedin's numbers increased with luminaries such as Dr Kiran Mazumdar-Shaw and Nandan Nilekani.

However, when it comes to politicians, they are still trying to figure it all out on this medium. What is the real way to maximize campaign benefits for politicians who may choose to get on to Linkedin? Hari Krishnan, Managing Director of linkedin Asia Pacific suggests that the key to the success of any campaign is relevance. 'Content alone will not be sufficient to drive engagement with audiences. Content that is relevant, and that resonates with the audience will go all the way and become viral. That means that understanding your audience is paramount.' He explains, that campaign engagement is not a 'on' now, 'off' later thing. 'It really requires a 24/7 approach to ensure you can interact with your audience in a timely manner, particularly when the news is not all positive. People want to know you are there all the time, not just when you need to get your message out, one-way.'

So, does Linkedin really matter? It's a great space to engage with people who can become executers of projects and campaigns and tap further talent to promote the canvassing efforts. Additionally it's a good place to do background checks on people who have volunteered or are keen on being part of political teams. It's a perfect networking tool in a more closed and controlled user group. Leaders looking to reach out to connections of connections who can either join in or support from outside, hold events and fundraisers are all among the professional networking embedded in this social media. Why not use it? 'I've seen many ways individuals and organizations use Linkedin to further their cause, including raising funds,' articulates Krishnan. He cites additional reasons for why politicians may benefit from it. 'By getting your message out and engaging this group of influential and affluent professionals, you are effectively raising the awareness or profile of yourself or your campaign. Over time, you will also build a loyal base of followers which can spread your message further. This base can be a key support platform when things are not all positive. Lastly, by interacting with and engaging your audience on Linkedin, you are in effect gaining actionable insights into what they care about, something that is very valuable and that can perpetuate a virtuous cycle.'

Just like Twitter and Facebook, Linkedin does allow its members to update their status, which could be locational, a viewpoint, or simply a new development. This updation can then become an engagement tool. Sharing public information, speeches, and rally highlights can benefit any politician willing to embrace this.

GOOGLE PLUS

India has seen tremendous engagement of Google with politics. The multinational is wired into the scene in India with the online space polarizing the debate on the future leaders of India. It launched an elections portal in India, giving voters a one-stop access point to all the news related to elections and politics, as well as information about various political parties.[19]

The elections portal acts like a one-stop point for users to read or watch content hosted by Google and YouTube partners and features links to Google Hangouts, which political representatives have held. Rajan Anandan of Google admitted at a recent conference that consumer and politics needed each other and that Google was only playing a part in providing a platform. Google believes this is a way of making sure that political parties are aware of what is happening with consumers and how they are using the Internet. The potential clearly is huge. 'There will be 240 million Indians on the Internet by the 2014 election, and that includes 70 percent of India's voters who can swing an election, search engine Google's India head Rajan Anandan said at NDTV's Solutions summit.[20]

Google's entry into the election maidan is also triggered by just how many people in India are suddenly discussing this. It's become a national obsession. As a political source shared, 'everyone has a political bone in India. It's just a matter of how much you scratch them to reflect their views.'

Google is already talking of using this medium for 'shaping democracy.' Chetan Krishnaswamy, Google India's Head of Public Policy and Government Relations, says, 'Our intent is to empower voters with all the information they need at a single destination for upcoming general elections. Over time we will add more functionality to enable users to interact and engage with the candidates, so that they are not simply watching from afar, but participating in, engaging with, and shaping the political process in a democratic way.'[21] Google's new elections section also brings people up to speed—albeit in a non-cluttered fashion—on how to go about voting, registration, and understanding the various forms to fill.

Google is aware that politicians are already using many of its platforms from Search to Google Hangout to drive engagement. Several political parties and politicians now have YouTube channels as well where they are able to reach out to millions of Indians.

YOUTUBE

YouTube is the world's second largest search engine after Google. 'With YouTube's global reach and ease of use, it's changing the way that politics—and its coverage—is happening,' says Steve Grove, YouTube's Political Director in a Harvard Neiman Report. And it's true. He pointed out how thousands of advocacy groups and non-profit organizations used YouTube to get their election messages into the conversation. This is beginning to happen in India as well. Video has become a medium of easy consumption. 'Visual content is social-media-ready and social-media-friendly. It's easily sharable and easily palatable. Images on social media get more engagement than links or text. Images on your website have a higher chance of being shared than anything else. In 2014, visual content is just smart business,' says Business2Community.com in an article.[22]

It's also a place where leaders can communicate with their constituents and control the messaging they intend giving out. For example, while news channels may pick one juicy quote and string it with other commentary, YouTube–savvy leaders are ensuring they put their videos out the way they want it.

For his campaign, Narendra Modi's YouTube channel (account opened in 2007) is pretty active. It has over 1,09,300 subscribers and 12,302,053 views. Modi's team has effectively used the platform to not only use this as a news channel on Modi but also carries videos on 'how to connect with Modi via social media' or his day to day meetings with different audiences. They update the video footage after editing it within minutes or hours of the event. After that Modi's entire army, which includes a large number of websites and handles, uses a particular clip to amplify the thoughts of the leader.

India272.com and NitiCentral.com are examples of volunteer platforms for BJP or the right-wing which are big on video push. On Facebook as well there are active clubs like 'Narendra Modi for PM' and 'Modi-fying India' that condition videos based on a planned message, an anti-Congress campaign, or hail their leader's activities. YouTube is a multimedia platform with the power to grip people. Videos also are among the most shared items across social media.

Indian politicians are using online videos for their campaigns ads, to broadcast official speeches and events and to tailor make messaging for people. Given the popularity of some politicians, they are able to successfully push it down social media and keep the hits high.

Grove hails this YouTube culture as an introduction of a new 'meritocracy', one that is 'unburdened by the gatekeeping middleman.' He calls YouTube the world's largest town hall for political discussion, where voters connect with candidates—and the news media—in ways that were never before possible.[23]

Video also lends itself to easy and quick consumption and therefore also urges more people to share it. In 2006, the famous 'macaca' moment triggered the arrival of politics on YouTube in the United States. US Republican Senator from Virginia, George Allen, was caught on tape at a campaign event calling a college student of Indian descent a 'macaca'—a word considered racial slur—twice. *New York Times* (NYT) reported that the clip once put on YouTube, 'rocketed to the top of the site's most-viewed list.' That was it. After that, most newspapers and channels picked it up. As Ryan Liza put it in the same NYT piece, 'When politicians say inappropriate things, many voters will want to know. Now they can see it for themselves on the Web.' [24]

In 2007, CNN did an article called the 'youtube-fication of elections.'[25] It shares the story of how the Obama vs McCain campaign multiplied its effect with video. Citing John McCain's YouTube moment in April that year, the article narrated the clip of McCain which said, 'Remember that old Beach Boys song, bomb Iran. Bomb. Bomb. Bomb.' That was the Republican presidential candidate having some fun with a friendly crowd in South Carolina. But his comments got played over and over again on YouTube and became a story picked up by the mainstream media, explains CNN.

The article gives another example. 'You cannot go to a 7-Eleven or a Dunkin' Donuts unless you have a slight Indian accent. I'm not joking,' said Democratic presidential hopeful Joe Biden in July 2013. The senator from Delaware was joking, but his comments made the rounds on YouTube, and Biden needed to clarify just what he was talking about.

In India, while YouTube has proved to be a solid propaganda machine, it also has got politicians making news. News that once captured tends to go viral. One such moment was BJP leader Sushma Swaraj dancing at Raj Ghat (Mahatma Gandhi's samadhi) in the capital of Delhi. Swaraj defended herself saying she was dancing to the tune of patriotic songs to boost the morale of the cadres, which is in keeping with the traditions of the party. She was criticized by the ruling government for humiliating Raj Ghat by 'dancing' there.

ComScore outlook for India's digital future talks about YouTube becoming an important power piece. The online video audience grew by 27 percent although majority of this goes into entertainment, more and more people are logging online to watch videos on politics as well. The medium is out there for people to use even more now that India is opening up to better telecom bandwidths.

BLOGS

Interestingly, no matter how ignored this category remains in a political sense, blogs have grown the most according to the ComScore report. With a 48 percent growth year on year, blogs added more than 11 million new users. Blogging is fast catching up as a medium to spread ideas because it is expressional and informational. It allows writers to be creative with the political subject at hand. Live-blogging, which entails putting out short snippets as things happen, is another fantastic tool for getting people to follow. Most interesting blogs can spur a solid following allowing people to keep up to speed with new and interesting updates about the subject matter.

The use of social media is becoming a feature of political and civic engagement. This is true for campaigns across the world. Social media is here for good, if not for the better. Politicians can no longer escape any of the media discussed above without being answerable to their voters. Leaders need to know there is no private life or down time for them any longer. They are being watched, tweeted, taped, or photographed practically everywhere. And by anyone. In the mid 2000s, YouTube's impact on politics may have been exaggerated but not any longer. The site's users are generally young and not highly engaged politically. One can say the same about Facebook. The medium may have a lot of people just talking about their dog's poo or the next best bridal shower but even most of these people are beginning to become a part of the social fabric of the online network. They want to be seen as opinionated people. They want to share their experiences on how policy, politics, and civic life affects them.

Just as social media has become an increasingly significant part of our daily lives, it has also become a growing aspect of political campaign. This self-imposed openness on politics is strengthening the network on the social Internet. And it just cannot be ignored. Jeff Jarvis, who runs Buzz Machine and is a media watcher, puts it plainly, 'We don't come to social services to hide secrets; that would be idiotic. We come to share.'

REFERENCES

1. http://ivn.us/2012/10/31/Twitter-in-the-2012-election-10-reasons-why-it-matters/

2. Read more at: http://phys.org/news/2013-09-Twitter-emerges-indispensable-political-tool.html#jCp

3. http://twiplomacy.com/info/asia/india/

4. http://www.businessinsider.in/Why-You-Should-Care-About-Twitter/articleshow/22864808.cms

5. http://www.theguardian.com/commentisfree/2013/sep/14/Twitter-flotation-facebook-politics-social-network

6. http://phys.org/news/2013-09-Twitter-emerges-indispensable-political-tool.html

7. http://indiatoday.intoday.in/story/narendra-modi-Twitter-typo-lotus-vs-louts-bjp-madhya-pradesh-polls/1/326162.html

8. http://www.forbes.com/sites/saritharai/2013/07/25/in-indias-polarizing-election-of-2014-Twitter-and-facebook-already-winners/

9. http://twiplomacy.com/info/asia/india/

10. https://blog.Twitter.com/2013/2013-the-year-on-Twitter-in-india

11. *Social Elected,* Craig Agranoff and Herbert Tabin, Pg, 59

12. http://videathink.com/social-media/narendra-modi-famous-politician-social-media/#_

13. https://www.facebook.com/notes/us-politics-on-facebook/less-than-100-days-until-election-facebook-offers-tips-for-campaigns/10150937198965882

14. http://www.niticentral.com/2013/07/17/the-curious-case-of-ashok-gehlots-his-turkish-likes-105219.html

15. (http://ibnlive.in.com/news/cobrapost-for-rs-92000-you-can-destroy-reputations-on-fb-twitter/436731-3.html)

16. http://maximizesocialbusiness.com/linkedin-for-politicans-281/

17. http://www.bbc.co.uk/news/uk-politics-15293934

18. http://www.linkedin.com/profile/view?id=103962395&locale=en_US&trk=tyah2&trkInfo=tas%3Anarendra%20modi%2Cidx%3A2-1-2

19. http://www.google.co.in/elections/ed/in

20. http://www.ndtv.com/article/ndtv-25-latest/india-will-have-240-million-users-on-internet-by-2014-who-can-swing-an-election-google-s-rajan-anand-458649

21. http://techpresident.com/news/wegov/24576/internet-giants-google-take-new-roles-indian-elections

22. [http://www.business2community.com/content-marketing/10-reasons-visual-content-will-dominate-2014-0717804-!qkNiE]

23. http://www.nieman.harvard.edu/reportsitem.aspx?id= 100019

24 http://www.nytimes.com/2006/08/20/weekinreview/ 20lizza.html?pagewanted=all&_r=0

25. http://edition.cnn.com/2007/POLITICS/07/18/youtube. effect/

5

Defining Moments in Social Media

The power of social media in documenting world events is enormous and in most ways it only augmented the coverage these events go on traditional media like television, radio, and even newspapers. Social web and mobile technologies have accelerated the rate at which relationships develop, information is shared, and influence takes hold. In the last four years, for many, social media has become an important source of news. While the credibility of some sources can clearly be contested, even news outlets have joined the revolution, often making social media updates an integral part of their newsrooms and broadcasts. News can also quickly get passed around the networks in ways never experienced before. Political and social landscapes have transformed. Today thanks to such technological networking, sharing, and liking, there is greater political awareness and organization, which has indeed rewritten the laws of 21st century communication. Revolutions have been triggered, common people have turned journalists, activists have been able to rally support for their causes by simply creating a fan page, politicians have been able to get up, close, and personal with their voters, and information is exchange with no holds barred. Such is the power of social media.

'My goal is to spark something within the reader and allow it to initiate an idea they then can grow,' said Warren Whitlock (@warrenwhitlock) of social media. He perhaps gauged the social power of social media—the movements, the civil society, the power of many instead of the power of one, the hunger for online democracy. Digital tools such as YouTube, Twitter, and Facebook have redefined activism and information dissemination.

In no particular order here are numerous events that broke on social media or went viral.

THE OSAMA RAID

In May 2011, Osama Bin Laden's killing was documented on Twitter a day before US President Barack Obama even announced it. A young technology consultant Sohaib Athar who lived near Abbottabad, Pakistan live-Tweeted the raid that led to Bin Laden's death. He had no clue about who was being killed in his neighbourhood. His Twitter timeline articulated the operation as he shared details of helicopters hovering over the region (something that was rather unusual for the quaint town). @ReallyVirtual, Athar's handle, reported the covert mission: 'Helicopter hovering above Abbottabad at 1AM (is a rare event)'. Later, Keith Urbahn, chief of staff for former Defence Secretary Donald Rumsfeld tweeted news of Bin Laden's death with—'So I'm told by a reputable person they have killed Osama Bin Laden. Hot damn.'[1] When it all got public, Athar tweeted, 'Uh oh, now I'm the guy who liveblogged the Osama raid without knowing it.'

BOSTON BOMBINGS

In April 2013, the news of the Boston bombings first broke on Twitter. Pictures, videos, and news briefs followed from the scene itself on Twitter even as news organizations prepared deeper reporting. Vine (Twitter's short video platform) captured the scene as well. Google added the category 'Boston Marathon Explosions' to its Person Finder tool, designed to help friends and family members locate loved ones during humanitarian disasters. Several people were able to reach out to each other on social media given the massive traffic on telecom networks.

HUDSON WATER LANDING

In January 2009, the Hudson Water Landing was the most prominent news that broke and spread via Twitter. When a US Airways flight 1549 hit a flock of geese shortly after take-off, stalling its engines, it had to look for a place to land. Pilot Chesley Sullenburger calmly glided the powerless Airbus and its 155 passengers towards Manhattan's River Hudson and it crash landed in the water with minimal injuries—right in the centre of the city. A handle that went by the name @Manolantern tweeted: 'I've just watched a plane crash into the Hudson river in Manhattan.' Another user used Twitpic to release a photo of passengers on the wings, writing: 'There's a plane in the Hudson. I'm on the ferry going to pick up the people. Crazy.'

THE ARAB SPRING

The Arab Spring remains the most stark image of people mobilization via social media yet. The revolution marked protests and civil wars in the Arab region starting from Tunisia to Egypt, Libya, Algeria and there on spreading to Syria and other regions. It used social media as a centre piece for information sharing with the rest of the world. There were protests by common people to topple the dictatorial regimes and in that effort, civil society and people used every online tool to get their message out even as some governments sought to gag the Internet. For the region—that shied away from technological leaps—social media helped collapse borders and allowed people to share their feelings about state regimes. All demonstrated using of social media as an organizing and mobilizing tool. The world was following the on-ground movements by following the Facebook and Twitter accounts of well-known activists. These reactions demonstrated recognition on the part of these leaders of new media's important role.

Take the example of the Egypt electionswhere voters, excited to have voted, posted images of their inked fingers on social media using hashtags like #EgyPresElex and #Egyelections to share and spread the word. From the revolt in the country to its election, social media brought the events of Egypt out there for the rest of the world to see. Such examples were seen in other countries as the Arab Spring spread through.

THE ROYAL ENGAGEMENT

Prince Charles' office chose 140 characters to put out a succinct announcement of the happy news set to hit Buckingham Palace. Although a formal statement was issued, it was Twitter where it was shared with the world. @ClarenceHouse tweeted 'The Prince of Wales is delighted to announce the engagement of Prince Williams to Miss Catherine Middleton —www.princeofwales.gov.uk'.[2] In some ways, Twitter has revolutionized global news delivery and consumption.

Later the news of the Royal Baby kept Twitterati active with over two million tweets sent out on the same. Clarence House (@ClarenceHouse) informed the world that the Duchess of Cambridge had been admitted to St Mary's Hospital, Paddington in anticipation of the birth of her first child. The official handle also used Twitter to announce the birth of George. '@ClarenceHouse Her Royal Highness The Duchess of Cambridge was safely delivered of a son at 4.24 pm.' *Telegraph* in the UK reported that the hashtag #RoyalBaby was used more than 9,00,000 times since the Duchess was admitted to hospital.[3]

There are plenty of news stories that went down in history thanks to the one-line headline or the short phrase in twitter style. Additionally the memorable images, that now Twitter often breaks, along with news stories go viral far before mainstream media can report it. Barack Obama's second term victory image with his wife Michelle hugging him took the twitterati by storm.

EARTHQUAKES

In 2008, according to Mashable, tweets from China alerted the world to the region's severe earthquake. These tweets were out even before the United States Geological Survey had a chance to comment. Blogger Robert Scoble helped spread the news, according to the site, by retweeting reports from people on the ground, before the traditional media could get a hold of the story. Mashable also reported that the Virginia earthquake news spread on Twitter faster than many people felt the shocks in real life. 'Tweets began pouring in from D.C. nearly 30 seconds before we felt the quake at our headquarters in New York City and well before any reports about the quake emerged from the media,' the report said. Twitter later revealed that more than 40,000 earthquake-related tweets were sent within a minute of its occurrence.[4]

Twitter, Facebook, and other social networking sites became an invaluable tool for millions of people caught up in the aftermath of the Japan earthquake. Reportedly even the US State Department resorted to using Twitter to publish emergency numbers, and informing Japanese residents in America how to contact families back in Asia. Relief organizations used Twitter to post information for non-Japanese speakers and interpreters to those seeking shelter and support. People during the quake used social media to inform people of their well-being given how many phone lines had gone dead as waters rose in the region. People used social media to post news about how serious the situation was where they were, along with images and videos, most of which were tweeted and retweeted several thousand times. Some of these videos were even picked up by global news channels and carried to showcase the extent of damage.

OCCUPY WALL STREET

The movement to protest against corruption and greed of Wall Street and those working on it was one that started and spread thanks to social media. Called Occupy Wall Street, this movement triggered an uproar online and was supported by people getting together in New York parks near Wall Street to protest the greed that had led the economy's collapse and hit the common man. It's Facebook page with over 4,50,000 fans used the medium to garner support and gather in places for protests. What started as a small protest, suddenly catapulted into mass crowds moving across Manhattan highlighting the disgust of people with economic policies and the disconnect of common people with Wall Street's wealthy. In an interview with the *Huffington Post*, Change.org founder Ben Rattray said, 'These tools are actually not that complicated… Social change is less about the tools and more about the applications of those tools.' Rattray added that social media is used for 'supporting, not supplanting, existing strategies,' though at the same time it can absolutely 'spark something that wouldn't exist,' he said.[5] Later Occupy Wall Street would become an inspiration for such protests in different countries including Greece where people were upset with the government's sudden desire to impose austerity measures in the light of an economic crisis.

LAW AND ORDER IN FINLAND

In its bid to be truly representative of its people—the Finnish government got online to get the peoples' opinion on some of its proposals on laws.

The country passed a law that allowed every citizen proposal that collects 50,000 signatures or more to be voted on by Parliament. Finland is among the most Internet-connected countries and so this was not only an online success but a democratic way of getting feedback on pressing issues. Not only did citizens propose laws online, but the government was also legally obliged to listen to and consider the voters' demands.

DELHI GANG-RAPE

The brutal gang-rape, assault, and death of a young woman in India put the spotlight on India's mindset and pervasiveness of discriminatory attitudes against women. A young girl, christened 'Nirbhaya' without making her identity public, was raped in a bus which she boarded with her friend to go home. The incident was condemned across the country leading people to come out in hoards to protest in public places, hold candlelight vigils, and seek—in a voice louder and bound like never before—justice and security for women. Thousands of protesters clashed with security forces amidst rallies and demonstrations. Social networking sites were used to sign an online petition condemning the incident, stressing the need for more stringent laws. Articles and discussions went viral.

This was modern India's wake up call. And social media was at the nucleus of it. The news flow around this remained a live wire from 15 December, 2012 to 10 January, 2013. The victim died on 29 December and that's the day the social media chorus peaked according to a Brandtology blog which concludes, 'Social media has been valuable in creating awareness about the case, highlighting social issues such as oppression of women and patriarchal values in India. The responses and reactions to the horrific gang-rape case highlights the power of social media to stimulate debate, invoke awareness, and change attitudes in order promote respect and protection of women in India. Perhaps for the first time, Internet and social media have been utilised as tools to inform and mobilise public support throughout India.'[6]

AAP MANIFESTO

In 2013, India's new political party Aam Aadmi Party called for suggestions for building its manifesto by launching an online campaign to get ideas from the common people. It kept up the social connect after it performed spectacularly in the Delhi elections by getting the second highest seats, soundly defeating Congress. When there was a deadlock in government formation, AAP sought a referendum via SMS and an online form on whether it should form the government in the state, with outside support from one of the parties that it had strongly and vociferously opposed and campaigned against. The party published an appeal on its website, asking people to SMS YES or NO to 08806110335, else to call on that number to share their views. It powered this up further by sharing the same on other social media and online platforms. AAP would safely be the first Indian political party to have triggered such social media buzz that forced the rest of the older parties such as BJP and Congress to rush to set up communication cells and social media workshops. AAP used social media not just to engage and inform but also set up a formidable volunteer base.

THAROOR IN THE EYE OF THE STORM

Shashi Tharoor was once the poster of Twitter but became its biggest victim in a way that his online presence almost always impacted his real life. In January 2014, his wife Sunanda Pushkar was found dead in a hotel room after a public Twitter spat with the alleged third person in her marriage, a Pakistani journalist Mehr Tarar. Sunanda accused the scribe of stalking her husband Tharoor and even called her an ISI agent. It all came into the public eye after Sunanda opted for venting her anger on Twitter. On 15th January, a series of emotional tweets from the Twitter handle of Tharoor created a flutter on the micro blogging site. They were all directed at Pakistani columnist Mehr Tarar, who had interviewed Tharoor. When the media contacted Sunanda, it emerged that she had used his handle. By the time Tharoor, who had been on a flight, landed in Delhi and discovered the series of damaging tweets, Pushkar had hit out at Tharoor in full media glare. Tharoor immediately issued a Tweet in clarification, assuming that his account had been hacked. But Pushkar started using her own twitter handle to vent out further damaging details.

Some of that lengthy exchange is shared here.

SunandaPTharoor @sptvrock

@MehrTarar the audacity of a woman desperaely in love with an Indian "please shashi dont make me go i pleaded and begged i love u Shashi"

SunandaPTharoor @sptvrock

@Funny_Deol @ShashiTharoor @MehrTarar sadly it's not the men it's the woman who hit on a man when the wife is out 2 get treated how gross

Mehr Tarar, on her own Twitter account, said Sunanda was 'out of her mind'

Mehr Tarar @MehrTarar

I have nothing to say to a woman clearly out of her mind. To be called an ISI agent, a stalker. I have nothing to add. Just shows who she is Tharoor has had many ups and downs on Twitter.

Another big one was the Cattlegate Controversy. Tharoor was no doubt the dynamic Twitter buff. He became the first Indian to have 1,00,000 followers. This number has soared to 2 million in recent times. In 2009, one of Tharoor's tweets not only made headlines, but cost him his job. Tharoor ran into trouble for a message he posted in which he said sarcastically in response to a query on the government's austerity measures. He said, he would travel 'cattle class out of solidarity with all our holy cows!' He left it open to interpretation whether his colleagues were all holy cows or cattle class was a reference to people in general. His own party mocked him, saying he was new to politics and perhaps naïve about use of such phrases. His political contemporaries took digs at both him and Twitter. Then BJP President Venkaiah Naidu even said, 'Too much tweeting will lead to quitting'. But now as a party, BJP has a large number of its leaders on Twitter. And as for Tharoor, after four years of this incident, he remains immensely popular on Twitter even though his fan base was beaten by Modi's 3 million followers just recently.

TEHELKA GOA SEXUAL ASSAULT CASE

BJP spokesperson Meenakshi Lekhi, in a tweet, 'partially' revealed the identity of a victim who was allegedly sexually assaulted by Tarun Tejpal, the editor of weekly magazine *Tehelka*.

Indian Express reported that by evening, the post was withdrawn from Lekhi's Twitter handle. 'Within a minute, I realized the mistake and removed the post,' Lekhi said when contacted by the *Indian Express*.'It was only partial (revealing the identity) and inadvertent,' she added.

Less than an hour later, however, Lekhi called back the *Indian Express* with what she called her 'official' reaction in which she distanced herself from her tweet. 'It was not tweeted by me. My phone was misused,' she said.[7]

MUMBAI TERROR ATTACKS

In 2008, merely moments after the first shots were fired across the sites of Leopold Café, Victoria Terminus, Oberoi Hotel and Taj Mahal Hotel, Twitter users in India, and especially in Mumbai, were providing instant eyewitness accounts of the unfolding horror. Twitter was yet in its nascent stage for the country. CNN reported, 'With more than 6 million members worldwide, an estimated 80 messages, or "tweets", were being sent to Twitter.com via SMS every five seconds, providing eyewitness accounts and updates.' The news giant carried interviews with people who said, 'Even before I actually heard of it on the news I saw stuff about this on Twitter.'

THREATS OF MORE ATTACKS

In 2013, Indian Mujahideen sent a warning on Twitter about attacking Mumbai leading to security being tightened. The Twitter handle @IndianMujahideen threatened to carry out similar attacks in Mumbai, while claiming responsibility for the Bodh Gaya serial blasts. Hours after the early morning blasts at the Mahabodhi Temple in Bodh Gaya on July 07, a tweet on the account had claimed responsibility for the attack, saying: '9 Dhamake Humne Karay' (We carried out the nine blasts).

While global revolutions, political spats, and controversies have occupied the minds and timelines of the social media user, the space has for long been where entertainment stories have broken, spread, multiplied, and gone viral. There have been some big examples lately.

LGBT RIGHTS

Social media has been at the heart of the debate over gay rights in India. These LGBT rights were discussed in India for the first time in 2009 under Section 377, which deals with rights for gay people. This was about four years ago. The word spread, people opined frankly, and ensured they were heard. But just as swiftly social media helped the positive vibes of a pending law finally taking shape, in late 2013, it erupted with anger at the Supreme Court's plan to reverse it. The section was declared unconstitutional with respect to sex between consenting adults by the High Court of Delhi on 2 July, 2009. That judgement was overturned by the Supreme Court of India on 11 December, 2013, with the Court holding that amending or repealing Section 377 should be a matter left to Parliament, not the judiciary.

The Twitter world helped spread the debate on the subject through the society's most influential, from ministers to activists, all of who expressed their opinion. Some highlighted how primitive India's laws had become over the issue of gay rights. Among the tweets that were significantly retweeted, here are some.

Nigel Britto: 'Won't judge gay people.'—Pope Francis. 'Not to worry, we will.'—Supreme Court of India. #S377

Chetan Bhagat: What?! Consensual gay sex ruled illegal in 2014? Shows you how badly India needs new young leaders with a modern outlook.

Vir Das: Today is 11.12.13. Unless you work in our Supreme Court, in which case it's the year 1826.

Rajdeep Sardesai: On his last day as a SC judge, Justice Singhvi got this one badly wrong. Badly.

WHITNEY HOUSTON'S DEATH

Twitter broke the news of Whitney Houston's death twenty minutes before the rest of the press. Mashable quoted data that showed the handle @chilemasgrande announced the news. The news of Houston's death spread fast on Twitter. In fact, about 2.5 million tweets and retweets occurred in the first hour, amounting to more than 1,000 tweets a second, according to Topsy Labs as quoted on the site.[9]

AMY WINEHOUSE

Amy Winehouse's death, tweeted just 20 minutes after she was found, was circulating on Twitter even before her father was made aware. Forty minutes before the story was reported on mainstream news websites and TV channels, and within 20 minutes of the police being called, Twitter users had already been retweeting early tributes to the 27-year-old singer, articulated stylist.[10]

MICHAEL JACKSON'S DEATH

News of the King of Pop's untimely demise in June 2009 was a TMZ scoop, but it went viral via Twitter. How did TMZ manage to trump the mainstream media, all of whom were camped outside the hospital waiting for official confirmation? Reportedly, the entertainment news tracker TMZ didn't wait for official confirmation but whatever the case, the news was lapped up by social media and suddenly fan pages, blogs, social media tributes followed in addition to mainstream news coverage. One estimate suggested that on the day of Jackson's death, tributes and coverage accounted for nearly 30 percent of all Twitter traffic.

Social media has become central to lives of people as the reach of Internet spreads rapidly. India is also one such country where Twitter obsession spread like wildfire. Its universal appeal, increased connectivity, and the freedom of expression that comes with it, has been central to its growth. This transformation, and the proliferation of phones into every facet of human life, has had a material impact on politics as well. The way the Internet is transforming the development of public opinion, civic engagement and interaction in the public sphere, however, is still a topic that is grossly understudied. However, sport news has been the spine of social media from the very start.

OLYMPICS 2012 AND SOCIAL MEDIA

Prof. Andy Miah of University of Scotland wrote in his piece for the BBC, 'As the Olympic Games enter their final weekend, the news throughout the fortnight has been dominated by what was taking place in one main venue—not the Olympic Park or the Aquatics Centre, but the Twittersphere.' The event's opening ceremony triggered more tweets than tweets for the entire 2008 Games. Facebook's 900 million users—more than the total population of Europe—shared photos and comments about the event.[11] Besides the fact that social media offered a larger audience, it was also linked with the fact that there was tremendous cheering online for those who didn't make it to be part of the celebrations or controversies. Live chats via social media were scheduled by the International Olympic Committee (IOC) itself. Players were tweeting during the Opening Ceremony. The IOC launched the Olympic Athletes' Hub that featured tools like the "Top Followed Athletes" on social media and the latest updates from the Olympic Games on Facebook and Twitter. Many publications called these the 'Social Media Games.'

SACHIN TENDULKAR'S RETIREMENT

Sachin Tendulkar's response to the trending #Thankyou Sachin messages is now the most retweeted tweet of all-time in India, according to Twitter India. He got three million farewell tweets. On November 6, 2013, the Board of Control for Cricket launched a campaign on Twitter to thank Tendulkar for his contributions to the sport. All Twitter users who sent a message of appreciation to @BCCI handle with #ThankYouSachin hashtag got a Tweet from @BCCI with a picture of Tendulkar, with a personalized message and signature in his handwriting on it. The master blaster retired from cricket as the world's leading scorer in both test-match and one-day cricket, and the only man to score 100 international centuries.

CRICKET AUSTRALIA'S TWITTER GAFFE

Cricket Australia was forced to apologize after being criticized on social media for a clumsy joke involving England spinner Monty Panesar posted on Twitter during the opening day of the second Ashes test. A picture of four men wearing turbans posing in a corridor was posted on the governing body's Twitter feed with the caption: 'Will the real Monty Panesar please stand up?'

SCREENING SOCIAL MEDIA?

In December 2011, India's telecom minister Kapil Sibal who recently got on to Twitter himself was once considered the medium's biggest enemy. His suggestion that social networking websites screen content before publishing triggered widespread anger amongst Indian Internet users. In fact, the hashtag #IdiotKapilSibal was one of the top Twitter trends in India that day. This story did get out of control as people trolled media against Sibal and his desire for 'supervision' of content. Google said that, 'When content is legal but controversial we don't remove it because people's differing views should be respected, so long as they are legal.' Facebook, in statement in response to the developments, said, 'We want Facebook to be a place where people can discuss things freely, while respecting the rights and feelings of others, which is why we have already have policies and on-site features in place that enable people to report abusive content. We will remove any content that violates our terms, which are designed to keep material that is hateful, threatening, incites violence, or contains nudity off the service. We recognize the government's interest in minimizing the amount of abusive content that is available online and will continue to engage with the Indian authorities as they debate this important issue'.[12]

The events mentioned in this book do not make for an exhaustive list. But these are a sampling of some of the biggest and game-changing events across the world that used social media. Given that people are now able to livestream political rallies and protests, tweet their opinions on politicians and political events to hundred or thousands of followers in record time, there is a new wave of information flow being experienced. Old economy media is reinventing to keep up with the time. Additionally social media is giving people a voice. You don't have to be 'media' to share or talk. These new online platforms are a megaphone giving a voice to people wanting to get their message out there, allowing for the articulation of new political discourses, social ideas, a new audience, and opening all to the others. These tools may have a positive or a negative influence but that's for a user to figure out. What's true is that the nature of social media is changing both the political and social fabric of information and engagement as history has so far known. Social media penetration itself is a revolution that has defied traditional ways of communication and threatened the very existence of mainstream media in different ways. With such widespread interest in the digital world, it forced someone to ask 'if a news event happened, but nobody tweeted about it, did it actually happen?'

REFERENCES

1. http://techcrunch.com/2011/05/01/news-of-osama-bin-ladens-death-spreads-like-wildfire-on-twitter/?ncid=dynaldusaolp00000255

2. http://voices.washingtonpost.com/celebritology/2010/11/prince_williams_big_news_comes.html

3. http://www.telegraph.co.uk/technology/news/10196618/Royal-baby-takes-digital-world-by-storm-with-over-2m-Twitter-mentions.html

4. http://mashable.com/2013/10/31/twitter-news/

5. http://www.huffingtonpost.com/2011/10/06/occupy-wall-street-social-media_n_999178.html

6. http://www.brandtology.com/blog/uniting-through-social-media-to-call-for-respect-and-protection-of-women

7. http://www.indianexpress.com/news/bjps-lekhi-tweets-victims-last-name-admits-mistake-then-says-someone-else-did-it/1201500/

8. http://blogs.wsj.com/indiarealtime/2011/04/29/omar-abdullah-new-twitter-star/

9. http://mashable.com/2012/02/12/whitney-houston-twitter/

10. http://www.stylist.co.uk/life/amy-winehouse-how-twitter-broke-the-news#image-rotator-1

11. http://edition.cnn.com/2012/08/01/sport/olympics-2012-social-media-london/index.html

12. http://ibnlive.in.com/news/censor-war-online-india-vs-big-brother-kapil-sibal/209320-11.html

6

BJP and Narendra Modi: The First Mover Advantage?

Narendra Modi is the most mentioned political leader on social media. He has 3 million Twitter followers. He is mobbed on Facebook, maintains a blog, and his website is set up in a way that every sentence on it can be tweeted as 140 characters without having to make an effort of copy-paste. It's tweet-ready. As per FollowerWonk, as on January 3, 2013 Modi had about 30,95,770 followers on Twitter and his social authority is 81 (on the scale of 1–100; where 1 is lowest and 100 is highest). On Facebook, Modi has 75,49,972 likes and 9,60,914 people talking about him.

This popularity has got Modi dawning a social media halo. With his active interest in new-age technology, Twitter, and Facebook, the chief minister of Gujarat has turned into a Pied Piper for the young brigade interested in politics or the political future of the country. Several first time young voters are taking interest and following philosophies of leaders. And this is most pronounced in the online world. It's safe to say that before Modi became a PM candidate—he became a social media phenomenon. With the rise of social media and the arrival of politicians on it, there are greater opportunities for direct communication with voters, and Indian leaders are beginning to use this as a way to interact with people. India's own socio-demographics are going through a bit of a change. These massive exchanges on social media, extreme to moderate views, liking and sharing, and then magnifying the message—these are also signs that from complete political apathy and disinterest, India's professionals are showing interest by actively participating to determine the nation's future leadership.

In India, BJP's prime ministerial candidate Narendra Modi is the most talked about person on Facebook, beating the likes of cricketing legend Sachin Tendulkar. According to Facebook's top Indian trends of 2013, RBI Governor Raghuram Rajan and India's Mars Mission also failed to beat the Gujarat Chief Minister, who was the most mentioned person on Facebook that year. Facebook, which at present claims to have 1.19 billion monthly active users (MAUs), has 82 million MAUs in India for the quarter ending June 31, 2013.[1]

With the transformation of the Internet, particularly since the first cyber boom of 2000, a lot has changed in the way information is disseminated. People are now able to live stream political rallies and protests, tweet their opinions on politicians and political events to hundreds or thousands of followers in record time, and spread information on issues faced by their communities across countries and continents with the press of a button. Just a like or a follow or a simple Google search can make you a part of the online social space. It's no longer on desktops—it's on mobile phones. It's not copious amounts of text but it's a short and snappy; there are infographics, Google alerts, websites, blogs, and YouTube. Smartphones bring you the world you choose to subscribe to. And this is a world where Modi has already been elected. He sets his own agenda. And more often than not, he himself drives it. What's that saying? If you want to get anything right, do it yourself because no one will do it as well as you. This holds true for Modi who has time and again said that social media can be effective in taking the party's key themes and messages to a wide spectrum of electorate, especially the youngsters who constitute a major chunk of voters. Sometimes Modi's clear distinction within the social media set also raises questions on whether those who admire Modi can automatically be considered BJP supporters. But more on that later.

India's Modi-wave on social media is driven by smart-phones. A large number of lower-priced models have flooded the market. From domestic handset makers to Chinese versions, smartphone sales in India has grown over three-fold to touch 12.8 million units in third quarter of 2013, cannibalizing the feature phone market.[2] According to research firm IDC, the India smartphone market grew by 229 percent year-on-year. From a taxi driver to a vegetable vender, in rural India or urban—everyone is hooked to their phones. Facebook is a big part of this rush for smart-phones, and it is possibly the one built-in or loaded feature that comes with nearly every phone on sale.

After a conversation with his strategists, it appears Modi sees this change as one that's parallel to the desire for work, food, and other livelihood needs. Cyber consumption, he believes, is central to people's lives in the 21st century. As articulated in his own blog, in his campaigns, Modi insists 'that the BJP as an organization is looking to creatively harness the power of social media. We have to ensure our youth stays engaged in our democratic process. We have to make our democratic process accessible to them. Social media is an important tool for this.'[3] India, as a developing nation, has proven such trends to be true to some extent. With access to new technology in a flat world, India has an advantage of staying ahead of the curve and so the country tends to leap frog revolutions. Take the example of the landline phone. India didn't see a massive proliferation of it. We jumped straight to the mobile revolution. Modi and other political leaders realized this early on and acted upon it.

Of late the party and its leader are both trying to use social media at every possible event and rally. It's first used for the run-up to an event, to build and trend hashtags, followed by an on-ground activity and reportage. Take the example of Bihar, where BJP was targeting almost one crore first-time voters. Ahead of his much anticipated Hunkaar rally in the state scheduled for 27 October 2013, BJP launched a massive campaign on social media to woo first-time voters in the state. Modi addressed the state after three years. Given that Bihar can have sway in elections, *India Today* reported that a '15 member BJP's IT-cell was working day and night behind the scene mobilizing support for the rally.' In Mumbai, where Modi held a massive rally at the Bandra-Kurla Complex, different media converged to give his campaign a bang for the buck. *DNA* reported, 'A toll-free number for registration, a dedicated call centre to mobilize grass-roots activists across Maharashtra, a social media blitzkrieg, online registration with a separate enclosure for such attendees and pick-up arrangements.' BJP social media cell convenor Jiten Gajaria told the paper that on the rally day, a special Twitter table was created at the venue to help social media volunteers tweet it live. This was also to be done for Facebook and blogs.[4]

To assert that people across the country are grossly dissatisfied with corruption under the Congress rule, Modi is using social media, number crunching, information, and images to share data nuggets on a minute by minute basis to drive home his point. No doubt, today the debate and discourse is being set in a sceptical world online where even the common man has the opportunity to make his or her voice heard. It's not difficult to find examples where mainstream news has been forced to pick up stories off social media and acknowledge factual intervention by those actively tracking their progress. Take the case of the debate on Article 370 and whether it was actually beneficial to the people of Jammu and Kashmir. On the microblogging site, Modi tweeted that he was glad that his comments on Article 370 at a rally were being 'widely debated among people and across TV and social media'. The mainstream media picked this up as Modi's view, notably, in stark contrast with that of BJP, which has so far favoured the out-and-out scrapping of Article 370.[5]

During the state elections in 2013, Modi made headlines with a tweet that took a dig at Congress' bad performance. Modi tweeted, 'The total number of seats Congress has won in all the four states today cannot even match the seats @ BJP4India won in 1 state!' He went on to credit the party members for the 'spectacular' performance in the elections and said, 'I congratulate Rajnathji, party leaders & Karya-kartas (workers) for their hard-work in the elections.'[6]

Luckily for Modi, the other parties—with the recent exception of AAP—have been slow on the uptake on social media and so counter offensives have been muted or sporadic. As Rajesh Lalwani of Blogworks notes, 'BJP is about the multiplicity of things that they are doing. For example, during Narendra Modi's Delhi speech, there were a large number of people present at the rally, but perhaps an equal number were hearing the live speech from their mobile phones and if you opted in to his Twitter feed, you could receive his tweets on the go. And so BJP—via Modi—has been able to scale up in a massive way, leveraging different digital formats and reaching out to a larger audience using social media. Its effort is clearly in reaching the largest number of people, across strata, in the shortest possible time.'

Although Modi's brigade is constantly questioning and deci-mating non-Modi logic, Modi has gone on record to claim that he learns from feedback and criticism. 'Social media is as much a medium for learning as it is for listening. Equality is the second cornerstone of social media.'[7] Some of what he calls feedback is also in the form of anti-Modi trolls, when he is the subject of brutal denunciation as well. 'I have been active on social media for over four years and I must say that my experience has been phenomenal. I have made several friends, connected with youngsters and benefited from the ocean of ideas and thoughts of these bright people,' says Modi.

If politics is about charisma and communication, Modi's oratory dexterity amplifies his image and his message. After building a digital friendly image, he has made use of his social media presence to gain mileage both online and offline. He now commands permanence on the web and his team— through various campaigns—is making it work for him. So what are the factors behind Modi as a social media brand? Brand consultant Harish Bijoor calls Modi a perfect brand. 'He is the epitome of everything a brand must stand for. He is loud, he is large, and he creates positive impact. NaMo is a lovely abbreviation as well. Easy on the tongue and easy on the recall. Modi is a four-letter word as well. Easy to recall. Very easy.'

Besides being a powerful brand, Modi has made every noise to assert the notion that other political parties are not social media friendly. During a rally in Karnataka in November 2013, he accused the coalition of attempting to restrict the use of social media, saying the central government knows it is a powerful tool in shaping public dialogue.

As documented by the website LifeHacker,[8] in 2007 YouTube was the first social platform that Modi befriended. His journey on Twitter and Facebook commenced in the months of Januray 2009 and May 2009, respectively. On 14 April, 2009, on the occasion of the 118th birth anniversary of Dr Babasaheb Ambedkar, Narendra Modi started blogging and he also had a personal website by then. Since then, the number of his followers and fans has surged. What's the story behind Modi? Why do people follow him? Has social media benefited his otherwise extremist image in the post-Godhra riots scenario? Was he a subject of bias in mainstream media? Bangalore-based Shashi Shekhar, who is the Chief Digital Officer for right-wing news outfit Niti Central, shares his three reasons for the leader's brand building. First is that he was the first major Indian politician who created a direct communication channel with the net savvy Indian citizens bypassing mainstream media. Second is his persona as a strong leader and what his rhetoric and politics symbolizes. He found a ready audience with the demographic that is most dominant in Indian social media—young, educated professionals who identify themselves more with the Vajpayee era BJP and centre-right politics. The third reason why he is such a strong brand is 'the overwhelming perception within this demographic of anti-Modi or anti-BJP bias within mainstream media. Modi has come to symbolize the empowerment of disenchanted mainstream media consumer who now believes he/she has a megaphone of his/ her own,' elucidates Shekhar.

Is this Modi's style of projecting himself as India's version of Obama? Has his team done a thorough analysis of Obama's work style? The numbers analysis has been core to Obama's win. Can Modi recreate that? All these expectations from the Modi brand makes one wonder if Modi will be able to convert his fans into serious votes. Voting is not done on the Internet. However, if the 21st century youth could actually vote 'online', politics would have looked pretty different. *India Today* conducted an electronic election[9], a mock online poll in which users were asked to vote in Lok Sabha constituencies across India through cellphone registration. One-time passwords were sent to mobile phones, and this ensured genuine voters logged in to give their vote to parties of their choice online. This mock election showed that of the unprecedented 5,56,460 votes that were cast over a 40-day period till October 30, 2013, nearly 3,38,401 users chose BJP. Whether this survey reflected the real mood or not, it clearly showed that majority of the people online are BJP supporters, right-wingers, or just staunch Hindus. Or as *India Today* concluded, 'the Internet is saffron.'

Rana Ayyub in her stint with *Tehelka* carried out a detailed investigation on Modi's online magic. In her article, she recaptured an anecdote that explains Modi's modus operandi and writes '...interesting anecdote of Modi's PR machinery comes from a journalist-cum-filmmaker working for an international publication. She wanted to do a piece on Gujarat and was given two dozen books on Vibrant Gujarat and Swarnim Gujarat. She was also given a CD with a video of Suhel Seth praising Modi. When she met the CM and his bureaucrats, she was taken around the office and handed over

12 books written by Modi (including those of his poems and compilation of his blog). "He's very impressed with Obama," said an official, "you should draw more comparisons between the two.'"

Ayyub's investigation for *Tehelka* suggested a less glamorous picture than the one painted by *India Today's* mock election. Her sources claim that a school called Sanskardham located in Ahmedabad is now the hub of Modi's PR activities. Members have Twitter accounts to post opinions in Modi's favour. She describes the Modi factory in this table in her article.

THE MODI FACTORY

The bloggers, students, and NRI businessmen who make Modi's slick PR machine tick.

DESH GUJARAT A web portal that widely covers Narendra Modi's public relation activities.

SANSKARDHAM Located in Ahmedabad, the school was an initiative of Modi before he became chief minister. It is now the hub of Modi's PR activities. Members have Twitter accounts to post opinion in Modi's favour.

NATIONAL INDIAN AMERICAN PUBLIC POLICY INSTITUTE The Chicago-based outfit fixed the recent trip of three US Congress members to Gujarat.

OVERSEAS FRIENDS OF BJP Convener Vijay Jolly was instrumental in garnering the Wharton business school invite for Modi, which was cancelled later.

NAMO GUJARAT A local news channel in Gujarat that focusses on Modi.

GREY WORLDWIDE The advertising firm that first came up with the Vibrant Gujarat concept.

THE BIG CONNECT / 101

APCO WORLDWIDE Replaced Gray Worldwide in 2009. Was responsible for the Canadian Prime Minister's decision to invest in Gujarat.

EUROPE INDIA CHAMBER OF COMMERCE Its convener Manoj Ladwa was responsible for lobbying for Modi before the British Prime Minister David Cameron's visit.

INDIAN AMERICANS FOR FREEDOM The goal of the website is 'individual liberty, free enterprise, and freedom from bureaucrats'. It gets its support from US Congressman Joe Walsh who wrote a letter to Hilary Clinton to grant Modi a visa.

HINDU AMERICAN FOUNDATION A pro-Modi organisation funded and run by Gujaratis in the US.[10]

With several examples to suggest that the social network remains dominated by supporters of BJP over Congress, it's worth looking at the people who are driving Modi's network operandi. What is it that makes him win online and, more importantly, who are these agents who are putting together this mean machinery.

MODI'S OPERANDI

Modi's men include a mix of those who are his nodal volunteers and some who are part of the BJP tech cell. Rajesh Jain and B.G. Mahesh—not a part of the party—are those who are supporting Modi's cause by setting up outfits like India272 and Niti Central; while there are others like Arvind Gupta who is heading BJP's IT Cell and is central to what information is shared on Modi and his ideology.

Rajesh Jain is among India's first Internet poster boys. He launched IndiaWorld and websites like khoj.com, khel.com, and even samachar.com. He famously sold IndiaWorld to Sify for ₹499 crore, triggering a dotcom rush in the late nineties. Jain along with a few others lead a 100-member content and technology team which sits in Bangalore to drive Modi's Internet campaign.

Jain has always had a finger on the pulse of the future. In an interview with Knowledge@Wharton in 2006, he put his bets on the mobile-internet world saying, 'Another dimension will define the future of the Internet in India, and that's going to be built around the mobile phone. Given the way that mobile phones have taken off in India during the past four to five years, I am convinced that more people in India will access the Internet through mobile phones than through computers linked to narrowband or broadband connections.' Six years down, it's the social media on mobile devices that's driving change and interaction. And that's what BJP is cashing on.

In a bid to consolidate the mandate received in the recent state assembly elections and achieve the magic figure of 272 in the upcoming Lok Sabha polls, BJP's prime ministerial candidate Narendra Modi launched a mobile application called 'India272+'. The mobile application allows volunteers to participate in open fora and share thoughts and ideas for upcoming speeches by Modi.

Rajesh Jain and B.G. Mahesh are known to be the two who are actively managing the work done by the volunteer-driven online planks. Niti Central.com is amplifying the signals and messaging based on their guidance on the themes of the moment as decided by Modi's core teams. Supporting these from the outside are other right-wing social media handles, websites, campaigns, videos etc. set up by Modi fans.

Call them Saffron Warriors. They are on the Internet, out on Twitter, taking on debates, and present at BJP rallies.

SAFFRON WARRIORS

Picture this. A bunch of unassuming youngsters are at a regular coffee shop. They look like tech professionals taking a much needed caffeine break. Armed with digital devices, a common thinking, a vision to follow, these gentlemen could well be there to crack the next big code. But are they? Ravi, Anshul, Ajay, and Prabhu are meeting for the first time but they know each other. Very well, in fact. They interact on Twitter everyday. They are up-to-date on each others' online activity and their one common interest is supporting Modi from the outside.

Not one but hundreds of cells like these have mushroomed all over the country. These are the Modi ghost busters, targetting at anyone who challenges the Modi political philosophy. You can call them internet Hindus, cyber Hindus, or the Saffron Warriors—their task is cut out and they do everything to protect the Modi philosophy, even if it gets personal sometimes. Taking a dig at a young journalist who wrote anti-Modi stories, the Twitter handle @internet_hindus tweeted, 'Leave journalism and become a broker or something. U have a bright future from 2014 when Cong will b opposition.' Mostly these Twitter handles are launched to be vociferous and opinionated. Their daily agenda is to pick the news, put up pictures and articles that criticize ruling party, and praise Modi or the BJP. They are the online crusaders who actively counter anti-Modi issues, while attacking the Gandhi dynasty with contempt and ridicule. So like there are party cadres who physically bolster the rallies, on the world wide web, there are the social media sanghis who multiply and amplify these.

Take another young executive @nitinkashyap, who on Twitter is a self-declared centre-right and hopes to see Modi as the Prime Minister. Of his 40,000 tweets, majority are spent on counter questioning others' views like: 'What does AAP stand for? Can you defeat Congress by being kosher? How come BJP ruled states better governed?'

Not only do some of these handles spew political venom, they also get recognition for doing this, by none other than BJP's Arvind Gupta. Praising a new volunteer, he tweeted, 'Absolutely proud of the way BJP Volunteer @sidgoyal1 handled questions on @NDTV. Represents the Passion.' The volunteer had represented BJP in a social media debate. It's this kind of acknowledgment and public respect that's also adding to the excitement of the youngsters who are volunteering.

Arvind Gupta, the head of the IT Cell of the BJP believes these platforms are all central to the party's overall plan. 'Volunteers connect to a political party in various ways. Traditional methods as well as technology enabled social media platforms both provide an opportunity for volunteers to associate with BJP. As a leader in this space, social media has naturally been one of the most important platforms for BJP to build volunteer base.'

Most of these cells work in sync with the party's head office at 11, Ashoka Road, or are closely monitored by Modi's own unit in Ahmedabad. According to the *Indian Express*, Modi's Officer on Special Duty, Hiren Joshi, reportedly manages a team of over 2000 people and is directly involved in Modi's social media messages including his tweets. Ahead of any event, Joshi plans and draws up Modi's comments that are later put on as articles or on Twitter. He is also the nodal man for setting his media agenda. With such an army of people working for Modi, there are some who are out in open supporting him, even if they are self declared right-wingers. And this includes bankers, journailsts and businessmen. During the massive pro-Modi rallies, in the different places of the country, volunteers numbering up to more than 100 from the local IT sectors are proactive in live streaming speeches, tweeting, blogging, and uploading images.[11]

An article in DashReview online asserts that the team behind Narendra Modi's campaign seems to have researched well. 'They have splurged content (with relevant keywords!) on all social media where it matters. They are on Twitter, Facebook, G+, some of the top social networking sites and they are in touch with the right set of influencers in the online world to extensively talk about Modi's campaign in the digital medium.'[12]

What's interesting is that they could well be college students or software executives, sit-at-home moms, many of who are who using weekends to work for Modi and contribute to public life. It's a part-time role they take on voluntarily and passionately. It is, as they may say, for a cause. It's that feel-good factor about contributing to the society's need for new leadership, the view that their voices are finally being heard, and belonging to a community of online activists who share their sentiment, which fuels their passion for rallying behind Modi.

Volunteers are coming from all walks of life to help Modi's campaign. Smita Barooah is a photographer by profession and a mother of two, married to a private sector economist. She took time off and left home in Singapore to come and campaign for Modi all through from January 2014 for the

May elections. She calls her decision 'a personal call to action.' On her Facebook post she declared to her friends, 'I am taking a sabbatical from work & my mommie duties. I will be heading to Delhi this weekend & stay till May to campaign for Modi...I believe that there are points in life when one needs to follow their heart & convictions. This is my personal call to action.'

These volunteers and those categorized as Internet Hindus may still be a tiny sliver of the total voting population, but given that social media is making people more aware of issues and manifestos—this community can ensure that the message is put across. Modi, no doubt, wants their help as he considers Internet and social media a tool for change. According to the Census 2011, 149 million first-time voters will come into the poll calculations for the 2014 elections, and so Modi cannot ignore what promises to be a significant constituency. Additionally, Modi and his party have rolled out a plan from multiple sides so that they are leaving little room for other parties to maneuver. From new Facebook pages, tweets, Pinterest, and scores of dedicated websites, there is a lot happening across the Modi plank. The goal remains one, which is to get 272 votes in the general elections. Shekhar aka @Offstumped explains, 'One must think of these different websites as constituting the 'Mission 272+ Digital Ecosystem' that are bonded together by a common purpose. Message coordination will eventually come as the Ecosystem starts to collaborate more. This is beginning to now happen with India272.com, which is the volunteer platform becoming the focal point for this ecosystem.'

INDIA 272 VOLUNTEER PORTAL - HOW IT WORKS?

INDIA 272
VOLUNTEER PORTAL

Through the India272 volunteer microsite you can show your commitment to the mission of helping the BJP get to majority in 2014 through your skills, contacts and enthusiasm.

What is more? You can do all of that while discovering friends, conversing with them and engaging with them to make this goal of 272 a reality!

TO MAKE IT FUN & COMPETITIVE, WE WILL AWARD YOU POINTS

Source: www.india272.com

INDIA 272

By its own admission, this website is an online and on-ground volunteering platform to help the BJP in its mission towards gaining a 272+ seat majority in the 545 seat Lok Sabha in 2014. Its face is Narendra Modi, the BJP's prime ministerial candidate and it is driven by the idea that people want to hear from other people what Modi is all about. The landing page of the website carries videos of volunteers sharing their reasons for pitching in. It claims to be the perfect place for crowd sourcing ideas and putting them to work for Modi. It's straight forward about its engagement with those who visit it and highlights, 'facilitating a one to one communication medium with candidates and campaigns as we get closer to the Lok Sabha election' as one of its primary motives. Videos with volunteers explain why they want to be part of the change in government and push for BJP's prospects. The website also features a BBC report on Anuj Gupta, a volunteer for BJP's digital campaign and how he quit KPMG to put his strong analytical skills to politics. The report cites the possibility that Gupta may be able to play a big part in turning around the nation.[13]

Outside of videos, the website has some interesting features including the option for fans and followers to upload hand written letters to visitors who come to the website. These come with suggestions, praise, and even poems. For example, for a Modi event planned in January 2014, the website invited people to register for a meeting with the PM candidate. But the meeting would depend on the work these volunteers have put in. And it did work.

There is a rather interesting element of the India272 website. It has a rewarding mechanism that creates competition within volunteers to do better and work harder. So a flowchart on http://volunteer.india272.com/cms/howitwork explains how people can garner loyalty points which 'give you bragging rights with fellow volunteers and also a measure of your volunteering commitment.' These points can be garnered when volunteers have something to show for their work online. So registered people can pick up tasks on offer. Some of these are translation of speeches that Modi has made, creating a catchy slogan, making presentations for BJP, writing poems or an anthem, and display creativity. For example, for a slogan, a volunteer gets five points and so on.

'The cyber campaign—started before the 2007 assembly polls through the BJP IT Cell—used to be a more centralised process. But the structure has evolved into a more decentralised and amorphous one over the years,' said Shashiranjan Yadav in an interview with *India Today*. Yadav is the former Vice Chancellor of Kutch University and architect of the BJP's cyber campaign in Gujarat in 2007. 'Now a large number of net-savvy BJP party workers and sympathisers are actively campaigning on cyber space largely on their own,' he added.[14]

The mediums are many but the subject at the core is just one. At the end of the day, no matter what platform, all media messaging is decided by Narendra Modi. He sets the agenda for all. He is intrinsically involved in the social media story. In December 2012, in an interview with *Economic Times,* Rajeeka Kacheeria, one of the few women involved in BJP's IT Cell, called Modi an 'amazing strategist—a good planner and extremely focussed.' She further explained how well the entire social network perception is micromanaged. 'Everything that happens on the Internet and social media is done under the guidance of Mr Narendra Modi. Hiren Joshi, a senior party professional clears even the smallest of our doubts on anything related to the net. It is not possible that conversations can happen as per the whim and fancy of a single individual. It's a collective effort.'[15]

THE NRI FACTOR

In 2011, as part of his campaign build-up, Modi realized the potential of engaging with NRIs and getting them hooked to his media and funding strategy, online. The Gujarati community is widespread in the US, Africa, and other parts of the world where they have thrived on their entrepreneurial ideas and hardwork. Modi in his own blog admitted to their contribution. 'As a matter of fact, NRIs are fast considering social media as their one stop for all the latest news on events back home due to its crisp and objective nature. Furthermore, they too are creatively responding by contributing in various ways.'[16]

MEDIA STRATEGY

Modi's content strategy changed as per his objectives, explains Ami Shah, Co-founder and Creative Director of IntelliAssist in an article. She follows his journey online and explains how Modi's early days of creating a brand identity involved sending posts simultaneously to Facebook, Twitter, and that the content revolved around inspirational quotes (his favourite leader is Swami Vivekanand), quotes from scriptures, and his daily activities.

In the second stage of building the brand, as Shah articulates, Modi became more focused on 'performance' and in turn built his 'imagery'. He started taking about his achievements and the developments in Gujarat; and his fans and followers had started engaging by liking, sharing, and commenting. 'In the third stage of building brand response, Modi's focus shifted on helping his audience build "judgements" and "feelings". This was the stage where Modi built his credibility, increased his consideration, and amplified his superiority.' Shah is quick to point out that none of this social media empire grew without a fair share of criticism.[17]

MODI OVER BJP

Modi's media strategy has worked independent of his party for years and during elections it needs to converge. There are some gaps in how the two can be integrated. Modi's team is focused on the leader and his achievements while the party's cell pushes party objectives with an eye on the elections. How does this two-way approach help both the party and Modi? Does it confuse voters? Where does it converge? No matter how hard both Modi and BJP are working to make them look like co-related brands, the message and the perception remains divided. The websites are too many, the volunteers in hordes as well, but what is the one binding spine of this entire campaign? Why do Modi and BJP need different sites? One can try and justify that Modi deserves his own platform but the two sites are almost disconnected from each other. BJP.org website is a detailed multipage with lessons in history, focusing on older luminaries of the party—somewhat disjointed with its current constituents—and has almost zero social media activity. Modi's own website narendramodi.in is up-to-date and centric to the causes he stands for. In addition to India272.com and several satellite-supporting platforms like Niti Central, IndiaFirst.in, Modi-Fying India, and NaMo For PM on Facebook are all working towards Modi. With so many websites and media planners—some on his behalf and some volunteers—the overall strategy is getting a little mixed up. This is somewhat different from the online management consistency seen in AAP and Kejriwal's website. Here, the objectives are similar, the focus is engagement and fund raising, and all of that is upfront and clear for the website's visitors.

The Modi platforms—a confluence of the official and unofficial channels—are all together overwhelming. After a few years or more of existence of all, one wonders which one is their official take. It clearly isn't BJP's website or Facebook page. Is it then the Modi webpage? Where should the potential BJP voter go and read about the leader they want to vote for? Does it make the task of campaign managers that much harder to sell and market the plan? Is this multipronged approach actually causing more clutter and confusion?

MAINSTREAM'S WRATH, SOCIAL MEDIA'S BALM?

Modi has faced the wrath of most of India's mainstream media. He has been criticized for being communal and divisive. Even now any mention of Modi's rising popularity is laced with mentions of the Godhra riots of 2002. Godhra riots was a period of inter-communal violence which broke out after a train carrying Hindus returning from Ayodhya was set on fire and that triggered insurgences between Hindus and Muslims. According to the official figures as reported by BBC in May 2005, the riots resulted in the deaths of 790 Muslims and 254 Hindus; 2,500 people were injured non-fatally, and 223 more were reported missing.[18]

From newspaper editorials to TV debates, Modi has constantly been at the receiving end for most. Even the United

States hasn't reconciled to giving him a visa to America, as a legacy of the Godhra incident. Such vilification has forced Modi's supporters to believe social media had the answers to beat mainstream media's notions or at least bypass it. 'The key difference between social media and mainstream media is that no single individual, entity, or agenda can artificially dominate,' says Shekhar. He blames the media for being selective and overlooking the rise of Modi, especially when it comes to Gujarat's development and business growth, and later his announcement as the PM candidate. 'The wisdom of the crowd ultimately prevails. In that sense it is a far more accurate reflection of how people feel about something than what one witnesses in Delhi's Television Studios.'

Modi's social media connect is embedded in the idea that he has embraced development in his state of Gujarat even though there are critics who have questioned the idea of development when divorced from human indicators. Modi's social networking skills have seemingly convinced his supporters and BJP's potential voters that he can replicate the success of Gujarat across India. Shekhar insists that the ground reality and Modi's persona are very different from what has been projected over the last decade. He adds, 'Delhi's Television studios have long ceased to reflect or represent the views of Indians across the length and breadth of the country. They are now merely an elitist echo chamber that have become disconnected from the real India.'

Modi has been labelled by the mainstream media as a controversial, polarizing, and divisive figure. Many prominent personalities have openly criticized him. Jnanpith awardee and acclaimed Kannada writer U.R. Ananthamurthy has said he will not live in the country with Narendra Modi as the Prime Minister. Amitav Ghosh went on record saying Modi remains someone culpable for the Gujarat riots of 2002 and he won't be voting for him. Nobel laureate Amartya Sen said he does not want Narendra Modi to become India's Prime Minister as he does not have secular credentials.

The online world has brought him support nonetheless. The proliferation of like-minded people belonging to the right-wing thinking—and this includes economists, journalists, thinkers, authors—are now able to take on Modi's critics in an open space. Additionally, there are several business honchos and that includes Ratan Tata, many actors, and national personalities like Amitabh Bachchan, Lata Mangeshkar, who have openly shown support for Modi or for Gujarat. Modi's Vibrant Gujarat, an elaborate business fair, was criticized for signing more agreements on paper than actually executing them. However it still remains a magnet for the country's top company owners who show up in big numbers for Modi's support.

Despite all mainstream criticism, Modi's strategists continue to boost his ratings online. Modi remains a demi-god for denizens who support his political slant. Columnist Aakar Patel in his article for *Mint* credits some of Modi's influence and status to the power of social media. He suggested Modi's fan base online has begun to act as a shield for him. 'It is not easy, and I would suggest it is not possible, today in India to put forth a view in the public space that is critical of Modi and not be shouted down.'[19]

There are also examples of converts, for example, journalist Madhu Kishwar who had a 360 degree change of heart about Modi after she attended an edition of Vibrant Gujarat, a mega event showcasing Gujarat's industrial might. Now she is one of his online crusaders.

TIMING AND STRATEGY OF TWITTER WARS

At the start of 2014, a few days ahead of PM Dr Manmohan Singh's national press conference, Modi strategists roused the social media world with questions for the PM with the hashtag #SpeakUpPM. About five of these questions then made it to the prime time TV hours, projected as 5 Questions Arun Jaitley seeks to get answers from the PM. There are many such examples. One of them is the iconic battle of Pappu vs Feku

Pappu Vs Feku

It's hard to chronicle a political discourse vis-à-vis social media without mentioning the Pappu vs Feku standoff. Considered as the battle of all Twitter trolls, new names were coined for Rahul Gandhi and Narendra Modi—that of Pappu versus Feku respectively. Gandhi's address at a meeting of the Confederation of Indian Industry in early 2013 first led to him being mocked as Pappu (dumb boy) while Modi's address a few days later at the rival industry chamber FICCI was spliced and analysed by anti-Modists who called him #Feku (hindi slang for liar). So the gloves were off, virtually speaking, for both the parties. The BJP came up with tweets to call Gandhi naïve and silly while Congress gave Narendra Modi the moniker of Feku for all his tall, and allegedly baseless claims.

Since then, the two hashtags have been around to refer to Modi and Gandhi by supporters or opponents. Rahul Kanwal, editor of Headlines Today in a tweet in April 2013 said, '#Feku vs #Pappu CII makes political battle more interesting. For long Modi's army has had area domination. Cong's belated challenge.'[20] The Pappu vs Feku fight was one of dominance (trending, in Twitter parlance) on timeline.

@JhaSanjay of HamaraCongress.Com congratulated his team for building the hashtag and tweeted saying: 'Team Congress, your feku was a stroke of genius.' At some point there came a time when Modi's people adopted #Feku and turned it against Gandhi. The @SanghParivar.Org tweeted, '#Feku Rahul said his father Rajiv Gandhi brought the mobile to India but did not tell that he was a middleman too #Wikileaks.' According to a website[21], the top hashtags for 2013 included Pappu and Feku. It's hard to say if both sides made very substantial points, certainly not enough to have valid empirical evidence, but the words—colloquial in nature—added to the media masala online.

With these hashtags, it was clear that the twitterati, trolls, and all put together were going beyond respectable ridicule with no limits to criticism, bad language, or fact check. Namita Bhandare in her article in the *Hindustan Times* discussed how this Pappu/Feku debate has crippled the possibility of moderate discourse in the online world. She picked two reasons for it. 'The first is the utter deterioration in the level of public discourse. While 140 characters are not exactly conducive to in-depth discussion, the virtual tu-tu main-main that has emerged over the last few days has both sides competing in the lowest denominator stakes. Feku is replaced by Internet Pappus. Abuse passes as comment. And on it goes.' She also expressed disappointment over social media universe which was meant to be a space for participative opinion. 'Subtleties of argument are lost. And those who occupy a middle-ground, impressed with neither alternative, face abuse from both sides.'

There are some iconic tweets or statements that have riled up the twitterati and put Modi in a spot. These promise to remain embedded in online history for life. As they say,

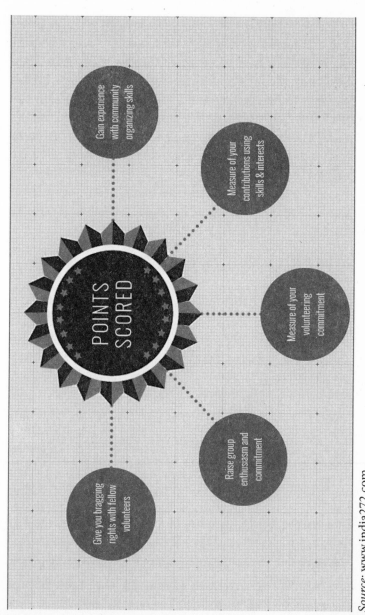

POINTS SCORED

Gain experience with community organizing skills

Measure of your contributions using skills & interests

Measure of your volunteering commitment

Raise group enthusiasm and commitment

Give you bragging rights with fellow volunteers

Source: www.india272.com

Google is keeping a tab on everyone. One such tweet was when Modi misspelt the BJP symbol Lotus triggering a wave of funny replies. He tweeted, 'Urged people to start voting early, vote for the Louts and give BJP a chance to serve them again.' Lout means an awkward brutish person, and this typo led through more than a chuckle or two on social media.

One area Modi has used Twitter effectively is pointing fingers at the current ruling government. During the PM's trip to Gujarat, Modi tweeted about state issues being ignored by Dr Manmohan Singh. 'We sought time from PM to discuss crucial issues of Gujarat including Narmada Dam height, farmer issues & floods but our request was denied.'

NAMO MERCHANDISE FRENZY

It's interesting to observe on how many counts Modi has tried to emulate the Obama strategy. As an extension of his social media and online campaign, he has launched NaMo merchandize. IndiaFirst.in and TheNamoStore.com sell anything from shirts to stationery and caps to cartoon booklets that criticize the UPA regime.

A lot of this stuff is put out on stalls during rallies and often volunteers and attendees of his events find it useful to shop on these sites and wear the merchandize to the campaign heartlands.

No matter what kind of criticism is thrown Modi's way, there is no doubt his social media aura is strong. Educationist and former Infosys member Mohandas Pai asserts the first mover advantage has them ahead of many other parties. 'First off the block, more organized, and it has more people on social media.'

WAYS YOU CAN CONTRIBUTE

Take up individual tasks

- Decide the amount of time you can spend in volunteering
- Choose your area of interest
- Select your skillsets
- Select among the list of tasks that suit your skills and interests
- Get your hands on at the selected work and earn points

Express your views to selected groups

- Register
- Join groups that interest you
- Enter discussions
- Share your views on important issues
- Tag friends by entering their email ids to make them a part of discussion

Participate in open forums

- Join Portal
- Look for any open forum discussion on a critical current issue going on in the portal
- Express your views
- Get more participative

Share on social media

- Running short of time but have something really important to share?
- Simply write your important opinion in the form of tweet in Suggested Post Section and share on social media

Mediawatch

- Scan through media coverage on web that you think is worth to be shared
- Add Mediawatch and let it spread

Earn points and badges

- Climb up the ladder of badges with points and the most active volunteers will get unique rewards !
- Selected volunteers will also get an exclusive chance to meet top leaders !

Source: www.india272.com

Political analysts may elude that tweets cannot bring votes and that Facebook is restricted to urban India. Given the fact that within the middle class, many a people have shied away or just stayed clear of voting, a social networking effort may at least improve the voting numbers of that constituency.

A nation that waits for their Prime Minister to speak up on key issues, the silent Dr Manmohan Singh's governance and mistakes have both done Modi a big service. Modi has used his speechmaking to garner support, promote himself, and even sought sustenance on social media. All this by keeping the pulse of the youth and putting his digital finger to work, and may be to vote?

References

1. http://www.ndtv.com/article/india/narendra-modi-trumps-sachin-tendulkar-raghuram-rajan-and-iphone-5-on-facebook-456646?curl=1386694512

2. http://www.livemint.com/Industry/53wbGwhSCE5SoRwGYsIiIL/Smartphone-sales-in-India-triples-to-128-million-says-IDC.html

3. http://www.narendramodi.in/narendra-modi-143/

4. http://www.dnaindia.com/mumbai/report-dna-exclusive-bjp-logs-on-to-social-media-for-narendra-modi-s-rally-1938544

5. http://zeenews.india.com/news/nation/narendra-modi-says-article-370-needs-rational-debate-bjp-defends-others-fume_893740.html

6. http://www.mynews.in/News/modi_makes_mockery_of_congress_poor_performance_on_twitter_N557769.html

7. http://indiatoday.intoday.in/story/narendra-modi-blog-india67-india-today-independence-special/1/298684.html

8. http://www.lifehacker.co.in/jugaad/Building-Of-The-Brand-Narendra-Modi-using-Social-Media/articleshow/28138520.cms

9. http://indiatoday.intoday.in/story/social-media-internet-cyber-hindu-twitter-narendra-modi/1/321267.html

10. http://www.tehelka.com/modis-operandi/?singlepage=1

11. http://www.indianexpress.com/news/the-men-behind-narendra-modi/1127260/

12. http://www.dashreview.com/digital-strategy-and-politicians-narendra-modis-online-presence/

13. http://www.india272.com/2013/12/10/bbc-reports-efforts-mission272-volunteers/

14. http://indiatoday.intoday.in/story/narendra-modi-cyber-campaign-cyber-activists-facebook-community-page-lok-sabha-elections-gujarat-chief-minister/1/262032.html

15. http://articles.economictimes.indiatimes.com/2012-12-12/news/35774026_1_social-media-cosmetologist-bjp

16. http://www.narendramodi.in/making-a-difference-through-social-media/

17. http://www.lifehacker.co.in/jugaad/Building-Of-The-Brand-Narendra-Modi-using-Social-Media/articleshow/28138520.cms

18. http://news.bbc.co.uk/2/hi/south_asia/4536199.stm

19. http://www.livemint.com/Leisure/fgP5yTgA1jCDji7VTmJj6M/Are-you-a-pappu-for-propaganda-doctors.html

20. http://news.outlookindia.com/items.aspx?artid=794859

   http://www.hindustantimes.com/comment/namitabhandare/the-stage-s-virtually-set/article1-1043465.aspx#sthash.WWHcIEvr.dpuf

21. http://www.mensxp.com/technology/web-and-social/21357-5-twitter-hashtags-that-defined-india-in-2013_.html

7

Congress and Rahul Gandhi:
Reluctant Followers

It's taken a while for social media to sufficiently 'poke' the Congress. Its efforts online, one might say, have always been a fightback. A reaction. A counterattack. It was never their own plan; never their own initiative. Mostly a 'me too' style. Congress didn't originally take to social media even though one of its own leaders Shashi Tharoor was at one time the most followed Indian on Twitter. Congress leaders considered the medium frivolous and dismissed it, often citing that votes came from rural India, and they weren't online. As the ruling party in the country, such an attitude fetched them no accolades. The party's image management took a beating; the party under UPA II remained shrouded under allegations of widespread corruption. For long, not having a clear PM candidate for 2014 hurt their communication strategy, one that didn't get styled by the young Rahul Gandhi. Not getting on to the social media bandwagon was interpreted as arrogance, especially since Gandhi gave no interviews to the mainstream channels either. Social media was one space where he could directly connect with his people but he chose not to. Has Rahul Gandhi hurt himself and his image in the process? And has he also brought further denunciation to the Congress with no leader taking charge on this issue? 'Yes, it has,' asserts Harini Calamur, the digital officer at Zee Media Corporation. 'Congress has lost an opportunity to engage, and politicians have to engage with the public in the new world order. If [Mahatma] Gandhi had been alive, he would have been on Twitter.' Rahul Gandhi not only failed to take the lead from within his party but also missed the bus on building a strategy and image as a youth icon, when it might have been in his reach, more than the other leaders he is expected to compete with. 'In the normal course, 43-year-old Rahul Gandhi and his youth "managers" should have been the natural mascots of this new India, and not a 62-year-old Narendra Modi and his sangh parivar. Rahul is younger, English-speaking, telegenic, and tech-friendly. And yet, as most recent youth surveys suggest, it is Modi who is the preferred choice of young Indians,' explains journalist Rajdeep Sardesai in his piece for the *FirstPost*.[1]

What also surprised many communication experts is that Congress has had enough talent to drive effort to reach out to the younger voters. With names like Sam Pitroda in their fold, who oversaw the telecom revolution in India under Rajiv Gandhi, it could have unleashed a social media wave if it wanted.

Of late the party has tried to shed its digital dilemmas and break into some planning. 'It is an irrefutable reality that social media is an emerging platform of the future that enables and encourages political parties to interact with people, get their feedback as well as engage on issues and programs,' Sanjay Jha, Congress spokesperson explains. 'Congress has more leaders on Twitter [compared with other parties] like Shashi Tharoor, Manish Tewari, R.P.N. Singh, Deepender

Hooda, Rajiv Shukla, Shakeel Ahmed, Priyanka Chaturvedi, Digvijaya Singh, Kapil Sibal, PMO India, Milind Deora, and Jyotiraditya Scindia.'

The party is focused now on adding more spokespersons, and training them both in traditional and online media. Ajay Maken, Congress' head of communications, participated in meetings and workshops in Kolkata, Jaipur, Thiruvanan-thapuram, Patna, and many other cities. Congress tweeted from one such of nearly 80 special forums: Great turnout at the Social Media Workshop at Baroda, #Gujarat today @ajay-maken @PriyaDutt_MP @Deepender SHooda.[2]

STRATEGY CATCH UP

The workshops and the effort may have come a little late given that Congress came on board social media after others. Why has the Congress strategy not been as effective as AAP or Modi's? Was it because it ended up following others? Does the problem lie at the top and its style of leadership?

The UPA II's political formation with twin power centres has caused many problems of communication and positioning of Prime Minister Manmohan Singh with respect to UPA chairperson Sonia Gandhi. It's anybody's guess who calls the shots. This is among the reasons why the young Congress brigade such as Sachin Pilot, Rahul Gandhi, Jatin Prasada and others have shied away from communication fronts even while being omnipresent. And this is when a young 43-year-old Rahul Gandhi holds the post of Vice President of the party. 'You can't be anonymous in parliament, give no interviews, rarely address press conferences, refuse high profile college fest invites, not have a Twitter or Facebook account, and then expect to reach out to a highly interactive generation which thrives on constant communication,' notes Sardesai in his piece.

Communicating in social media requires one to be transparent and quick on one's feet, which hasn't been a hallmark of the Grand Old Party of India. The challenge lies with the party 'structure', now made famous by Rahul's own criticism, which has always come in the way of information dissemination. 'What I feel is that this country needs to look at the fundamental issues at hand, the fundamental political issue at hand is that our Political system is controlled by too few people and we absolutely have to change the way our political system is structured, we have to change our Political parties, we have to make them more transparent, we have to change the processes that we use to elect candidates,' he said in his first TV interview with TimesNow. He further added, 'I think what the Congress Party needs to do is tap its potential, what the Congress party needs to do is change the way its organization is structured and look at changing the way politics in this country is structured, that is where I think we should head.'

The high command and control style doesn't work in social media as it is pretty much self-guided by those who use it. Did this go against the very grain of the politics of Congress? Why did it take so long for the party to pick up the pieces and set the plans straight? Dilip Cherian of Perfect Relations believes the Congress played catch up on the communications game, and that later it became too late to change. 'I think it is primarily now a prevailing mindset that nothing the Congress does seems good enough. The disillusionment with the ruling Congress has become deep-seated. Notwithstanding anything that they attempt to do, the cynics will criticize.'

Sanjay Jha contests this thinking and insists that young Gandhi's arrival online is just a matter of time and mind space. 'Mr Rahul Gandhi will take to the social media, like Twitter, when he is ready to give it his personal time and attention, unlike others who delegate it to a staff team. He is fully aware of the importance and relevance of the same.' But of late there has been some criticism targeted at Jha himself. An article on Rediff.com authored by Renu Mittal insisted that bringing an 'outsider' like 'Jha to address media persons from the AICC platform, the Congress party is not helping its case in regaining the ground it has lost in the perception battle.' Jha is the founder of Hamaracongress.com and speaks on many debates as a defacto spokesperson of the party, although, as the article said, he is not a member of the AICC.[3]

On the social media front, even as the Congress slacked, the Prime Minister's Office finally took the lead—only after a dynamic TV journalist Pankaj Pachauri joined the PM as his media advisor. Pachauri's move had an impact. The PMO handle's following shot up immediately. But it did appear that his ability to make the handle interactive is limited. Further, the PM's handle was criticized for its confused style of tweeting. It sometimes endorsed party decisions even though the handle belonged to the institution of the Prime Minister's office. Note that Jha considers @PMOIndia's social media strategy as part of the Congress' in a quote above. This not only drew flak but also led people to believe that strategic thinking was missing in Congress' approach to social media. T.V. Mohandas Pai, former Infosys member and now a civil society leader in his own right, feels that the communication is confused and worse, it's hurting the Prime Minister's image. He believes the demarcation between PMO and the party must be sacrosanct. 'We are not ready for a PMO which is more polarized as it then becomes the subject matter of ridicule and abuse, which could lower the dignity of the office. Maybe he should have a separate handle for his party work,' he explains.

Pachauri contests this with global examples. He says the WhiteHouse is the official handle and yet 'bludgeons the republican discourse'. He further explains, 'If the PM of India says something about Modi, RG and it is on record, then our job is to put in on record. WhiteHouse account is commonly bludgeoning republicans. It has nothing to do with Barack Obama. We don't do it enough in India. You look at White House or even Kremlin. On political things they are more vocal. We are instead understated. Because that's how our PM is.'

The party needs to move beyond a one-way style of communication. It's been apparent that the PMO wants to share only what it wants to share. Somehow the feedback aspect of social media has been missing. After all, social media is built on the premise of participative communication.

BEYOND HIT AND TRIAL

After some of these hit and trial methods, the party on its own began to recognize that it needed a more structured approach in late 2012. At one point the party that had dismissed the digital bandwagon saying that rural voters—perhaps the bigger chunk of the total vote—weren't wooed by it, suddenly felt the need to embrace it. Congress started to adopt corrective measures even as 2013 progressed. Priyanka Chaturvedi, a Congress spokesperson admitted in her piece for the *DNA*, 'While one can never predict electoral behaviour and outcomes, the number of Internet users in rural India might come as a surprise to some of these naysayers.' Another signal of the change in approach of the party.[4]

Several reports on Internet usage only cemented the idea that the digital campaigns were going to influence if not decide votes. And numbers were beginning to support this. By June 2014 Internet users in rural India will cross 85 million and active Internet users will grow to 56 million. Around 61 percent or 25 million of active Internet users will access the Internet at least once a week, said the report titled, 'Internet in Rural India' by the Internet and Mobile Association of India (IAMAI) and IMRB.[5]

Things began to see some change as the party realized it was time to take a digital leap. And this was further propelled by the success of AAP in assembly elections of December 2013 where clearly urban voters—also pushed by social media—played a big role in putting out a record turnout for voting. Efforts were being put to work slowly and steadily from earlier on in 2013. This was also when Rahul Gandhi started seeing and gauging the benefits as well as the spread of social media in India.

The Congress party began the year thinking of ways to sound and project themselves in a cohesive way to its audience. Whether Congress' stronghold is maintained in rural India or not, one thing became apparent to the party that perception was being built and created in urban centres, and that social media and Internet were principal to it. And thus began a series of workshops, some to train and others to review the way Congress approached media as a whole.

In August-September 2013, the Congress party took an aggressive strategy with a five-day special workshop to train its staff with mock television debates, group discussions, and lecture sessions by experts. Rahul Gandhi dipped in and out of these and reportedly explained the need for spokespersons to counter opposition propaganda with facts and figures. He picked up the Congress' marquee issues such as Food Security Bill and Direct Benefit Transfer schemes and insisted that party folks should highlight the Congress' strengths in all debates. PTI reported that over 60 selected party men from various states were trained in various subjects ranging from domestic politics, economy, and international relations.[6] Congress had also organized a two-day media session in July 2013 to tone up the party's communication strategy. It had also, on 23 August of the same year, organized a one-day workshop dedicated to social media. Both those workshops were addressed by Rahul Gandhi. So the beginning of 2013 saw the party embrace media education in a big way. 'The Congress party looks forward to greater diversified participation even from our various regional and state leaders and offices in social media going forward as greater Internet penetration and smartphones usage are likely to make India, in the foreseeable future as the largest market for social media. The young are now using the Internet more from phones than the personal computer,' explains Jha.

Jha, an advocate of two-way communication and personal engagement, did try to get more and more leaders hooked on to social media. But despite these efforts and open interactions within the party, not all leaders have understood the idea of social networking—that it takes two to tango. Take the example of spokesperson Manish Tewari who has a verified account on Twitter. He has about 17,000 followers but at the time of writing this book, he did not follow a single one. Not even his own party handle or the PMO's. Tewari has only given out information in his tweets, but has never tweeted to any-one or mentioned anyone in his tweets. This is also true of the verified account of the Indian National Congress—no replies to anyone, no interactivity, only informative tweets. This does lead one to question whether doing so implies a closed culture where they seek no news, information, or engagement?

As the ruling government maintains a one-arm's distance from social media, does it make Congress appear too glum? As an incumbent at the centre, are they likely to remain the butt of brickbats in the media for non-performance? Social media journalist Kunal Majumder believes that this could be a part of the issues but insists that Congress' entry into the medium remains confused and vague regarding a cohesive strategy. 'To begin with, Congress woke up to social media much later than BJP. Secondly, Congress' strategy is not centralized like BJP's. Thirdly, Congress is more defensive than BJP. Fortunately or unfortunately as an incumbent, Congress has the natural disadvantage. Most of its strategy seems to surround countering BJP. Unlike BJP, Congress leaders are still sceptical to the idea of social media. The reason Congress has not been able to become serious to this new platform is because RG still thinks it is a hollow noise chamber.' Shiv Visvanathan, a professor at O.P. Jindal Global University, concurs with that view, 'No doubt BJP's handling of social media has been far more sophisticated than Congress.'

CONGRESS VS OTHERS

The stark success of AAP via social media has left older main-stream political parties scrambling for strategy. Irrespective of the volatile highs and lows of the party's attempt at ruling Delhi, it's social media strategy must be lauded. AAP unlike most other parties used social media as a two-way exercise. Both, Arvind Kejriwal (AAP leader) and his social media handles for the party keep their fans engaged by retweets, replies, and also follow others. They have realized, that whatever the case, social media remains a two way street, and that's the bedrock of the game. US President Barack Obama follows over 6,00,000 people. UK PM David Cameron follows over 300. In India, where our politicians are learning the ropes of social media and experimenting with it, it would behove them to personalize accounts, connect at an individual level, and even share anecdotes. In Congress' case while the Gandhi family stays clear of social media, leaders in the party must use the opportunity to make up for that loss. But do they? There is, once again, criticism that Congress' leaders and the party's own handle are not well integrated at all. That is leaders of the party are somewhat disconnected from official strategy. Milind Deora follows fellow leaders like Pallam Raju, Jay Panda, and Naveen Jindal, but he doesn't follow the official handle of the Congress @INCIndia. Shashi Tharoor is often seen tweeting articles and posts from other media organizations even if its about other Congress leaders, not necessarily towing the official handle

Such disconnects must be addressed by a more intercon-nected social strategy as the medium is here to stay. There is no doubt that it is also becoming key to garnering political capital, especially among the youth. That takes us to the next impor-tant question—should party handles be quick in keeping up with the communication? 'Extremely important,' says Pai, 'as social media has become the instantaneous catalyst for news and opinion which works to shape general opinion. If chatter on social media becomes negative then it is more difficult to turn things around. Communication should be rapid and suc-cinct.' Jha and Congress both seem to be cognizant of this new digital reality. 'Naturally, the Congress party is keen to leverage the opportunity to talk with the rising young population of India, best defined as India's demographic dividend,' says Jha.

It's still hard to ascertain where the voters really lie and if social media alone can win elections, but that can be no reason to discount it. Several leaders have been asked as to why Congress' top leaders avoid the media. Shashi Tharoor in an interview with Reuters said, 'A number of workshops are being conducted. So yes, we are trying to educate party workers and party sympathizers who are interested in how to use social media constructively. And frankly, I think it's already begun, in many ways, to show an impact.'[7]

The Congress has been working on a three-point blueprint according to Priyanka Chaturvedi, as expressed in her column for *DNA*. One, to use social media to denounce propaganda of its opposition parties and its members, including Modi, who constantly takes a dig on the Gandhi family. Two, convince the undecided voter to support the policies and programmes of the Congress party and the UPA government. And three, use social media to convert supporters and volunteers into party workers. Chaturvedi insists, 'The enthusiastic response from our online supporters to these workshops has been humbling. It has also convinced us that we are working on the right lines in connecting with people,' explains Chaturvedi

Chaturvedi further talks of the communications structure of the Congress and how it works. It has a strong communication team headed by party General Secretary, Ajay Maken, supported by party Secretary, Priya Dutt. This nerve centre of communications is backed by the social media team headed by Deepender Hooda, the research wing headed by Sandeep Dikshit, and various spokespersons. The same model is being replicated in all Pradesh Congress Committees, and will then be rolled out at the district level, she asserts.

One wonders if this structure appears to have too many people in the social media scene? Does it help having a centralized communication plan? This means that while everyone is taking a shot at it, the party lacks a leader like Arvind Kejriwal or Modi, who in effect lead their campaign online; they are the de facto mouthpiece and therefore the newsmakers. This is over and above the core challenge that Congress' own official handles are barely 'interactive' and that its leaders are not unified.

'Mr Modi and BJP are doing a good job of the same [social media campaigning]. AAP has reached out to the voters much more effectively. Congress needs to think on how differently they are can reach the voter. It's a bit late in the day to suddenly do that,' insists Kiran Mazumdar-Shaw, the founder of Biocon and a member of the civil society in an interview on TV. Therefore the by-question of this is, 'How can Congress be a progressive party if they don't know how to communicate to the 21st century voter?'

The Congress has had a very successful social media star in Shashi Tharoor. He, in a Reuters interview, was quoted as saying that he tried to convince the Gandhis on more than one occasion to join [social media]. He said, 'This has to be left to the individuals in the sense that what their interests are, will often condition or determine what they tend to do. There's no doubt to my mind that both the Gandhis tend to be fairly reticent when it comes to projecting themselves individually; they prefer to let their work talk for them. I don't think I can persuade them to be anything other than what they wish to be.'

Jha defends this differently. He calls the Congress social media strategy an umbrella one with long-term goals. 'Unlike the BJP, which has a major cyber-army force recruited on a paid-basis to spread their divisive ideology, or indulge in malicious propaganda (exposed by Operation Blue Virus), the Congress party gets its support from volunteer-supporters, who are interspersed all over the country and abroad,' says Jha.

INDIVIDUALS DRIVE DENIZENS

Not being on social media with your own handle comes with challenges. For example, the problem with not being on Twitter is that when you trend, there is hardly enough of a mass to defend you. Pai calls social media 'people-centric' and hence he explains that just having the party or other people defend you, is not enough. 'The individuals in question should be on the social media dais to debate or defend in a transparent manner.' Today the Twitter trolls against the Gandhis are countered by Sanjay Jha, Priyanka Chaturvedi, Ajay Maken, or perhaps, even Digvijay Singh. But when Rahul Gandhi makes a political gaffe, the right-wing majority on social media rises together to make him trend for the wrong reasons. From 'escape velocity' to 'bee hives', his speeches have been thrashed by the online majority. This is one of the reasons why Congress is criticized for its strategy. Gandhi's rare public appearances and speeches mean that there is a huge interest in what he says when he does speak. Where it hurts his and the Congress' image is when the debate circles more often around 'how he says' what he thinks about the economy, political issues, social challenges, and what his solutions are for these if he were elected as the Prime Minister.

Rahul Gandhi's first individual TV interview with Arnab Goswami of TimesNow is a good example. Social media was flooded by jokes on the televised interaction. Some went to ask if Gandhi had lost the Lok Sabha elections after this. Gandhi was criticized for dodging key questions and responding to majority of the queries with a standard reply that emphasized the Congress' contribution to women empowerment, Right to Information Bill, and the use of the word Fundamental. Tweets such as these went viral.

"#RahulSpeaksToArnab used the word #fundamental 103rd time already! Fundamental waste of time, how's Arnab not losing his cool" tweeted @anandish

@rishibagree tweeted "If Stupidity was measured in bricks, Rahul Gandhi would be the great wall of China."

That this interview was a PR fiasco isn't something one could learn only from Twitter. It was widely talked about in mainstream media too. But there's no doubt the criticism Gandhi got came from none other than social media. The party learnt some lessons from the untimely wrath this 90 minute interview brought with it. *India Today* reported the Congress had realized this was a disaster and that in future Gandhi would undergo mock sessions, before any TV interview, by senior congress leaders. It also said Congress vowed that Gandhi's future responses would be such that they don't focus on an event but Congress' 'philosophy and ideology'.[8]

No matter how much the Congress members on Twitter tried to defend this interview, the fact that Gandhi wasn't on the microblogging site himself ought to have had an impact. And this is only one example.

In April 2013, at the annual CII Annual General Meeting, where young Gandhi was invited to speak about his economic perspective, he made an innocent speech and said millions of Indians were brimming with energy. 'People call us an elephant... We are not an elephant...we are a beehive... it's funny but think about it. Which is more powerful? An elephant or a beehive?' His choice of insects and animals was enough to tickle Twitter, where people went after him like stinging bees. Some called him a beehive of 'buzzing thoughts' and then there were others like this one from @ UnrealTimes, 'Manmohan Singh renames himself as Honey Singh after Rahul Gandhi calls India a beehive during #CII address via @ashwinskumar'.

This event was a sort of a watershed in the hashtag wars because it gave birth to #Pappu. The hashtag was used by all anti-Rahul Gandhi tweeters during the CII speech to suggest that the young scion was a 'dumb kid.' This gathered momentum significantly over the next few months with both Congress-Gandhi and BJP-Modi supporters crossing swords in 140-character phrases.

The once self-proclaimed soldier of the tribals, Gandhi, was caught on the wrong foot speaking at another event of the Dalit Resource Centre at Allahabad. 'Poverty is just a state of mind. It does not mean scarcity of food, money or material things. If one possesses self-confidence then we can overcome poverty.' This erupted into a controversy throughout social media. Here's a sampling of some. @Kesar_ tweeted on 6th August, 2013: 'Stages of #pappu's stupidity: > Rani ki Jhansi > Guj > UK > India = Thought > India = beehive > Poverty = state of mind #YoRahulSoDumb' Another tweet mocked the definitions laid out by Rahul Gandhi: 'Poverty (State of Mind). Wealth (State of Mines). #RahulDefinitions'.

Gandhi's challenge is not restricted to the fact that he is missing from the microblogging site, but that his party leaders too have done more than their bit to stir controversy via tweets or at least kept Twitter busy with reasons to criticize the ruling party and its leaders. For example, amongst the

Congress leadership is senior leader, Digvijaya Singh. His appetite for making controversial statements was in full display when he called fellow Congress member Meenakshi Natarajan, '100 Taka Tunch Maal'. 'She is very hardworking. She has done good work in Mandsaur and has impressed people in Delhi too. Sonia Gandhi and Rahul Gandhi like her. Not only that, she is 100% tanch maal,' said Singh at a public rally. He was ripped apart for using such language to describe a fellow colleague. Importantly several women's groups thought it was derogatory. Uploading the link of his speech, he courted Twitterati into a debate. Singh's tweet says 'Link of my Mandsaur speech and my comments about Meenaxi Natrajan. Are they SEXIST?'

Another controversy was sparked by Digvijaya Singh over the tragic Bodh Gaya blasts. He tweeted, 'Amit Shah (BJP general secretary) promises a grand temple at Ayodhya. Modi addresses Bihar BJP workers and asks them to teach Nitish (Bihar CM) a lesson... next day, bomb blasts at Mahabodhi Temple at Bodh Gaya. Is there a connect? I don't know.' In response, BJP claimed that Digvijaya had lost his balance and was trying to establish unnecessary connections. Digvijaya targeted Modi and linked the blasts with BJP. He tried establishing a connection by accusing BJP of targeting Muslims.[8]

However, courting controversies also reflects a learning curve. Four years ago, Shashi Tharoor's cattlegate comment—a sarcastic comment on the Congress' own austerity drive—on Twitter made headlines on all news channels. As the then Minister of State for External Affairs, Tharoor said in a tweet that he would travel 'cattle class' in solidarity with all our 'holy cows', Congress spokesperson Jayanthi Natarajan said the party strongly disapproved of the expression 'cattle class', purportedly a reference to flying economy.

More recently, Kapil Sibal's debut on social media was not smooth either. Kapil Sibal finally made it to Twitter, a few days ahead of Delhi elections at the end of 2013. His first tweet got everyone chuckling. 'Here I am. One of you. Let's talk.' To which he got back tweets like '@zaahidf @KapilSibal Pls give me your number; we can then talk!'

Times of India reported a debut faux pas of the senior Congress leader. It said Sibal initially followed a Twitter handle called @CommunalCongress, perhaps erroneously. But a little later and following some tweets highlighting this, his 'Following' count again read zero.[9]

During elections and beyond, the virtual wars promise to grow more heated. No matter if and when the Gandhi scion comes to partake the social media action, the concern will then be—whether he would be able to benefit his and the party's image with a delayed entry? The good news is that the party has its strategy in place. 'Our Official Twitter handles and other support-groups who have created their own pro-Congress websites and Facebook etc are now effectively disseminating information. The new-look Indian National Congress website www.INC.in, has received fantastic response already. Besides live tweets, we are web-casting speeches, uploading videos on YouTube and participating in Google Hang-outs and other chat-based platforms,' says Jha.

The government and the Congress now seem considerably energized for more digital digestion. In January 2014, apparently taking a leaf out of Aam Aadmi Party's strategy, the government considered making it mandatory for Union ministries to elicit public opinion before framing legislations. 'The proposal requires all central ministries to elicit public views on legislations they want to frame. However, no final view has been firmed up so far,' a senior government functionary told PTI.[10] This has been the main strategy of the AAP and it has employed it successfully, which was reflected in its stunning performance in the recent Delhi assembly polls.

With the stage set by the Congress, when can we expect Gandhi to walk the online red carpet? More importantly, will he manage to catch up with or outdo Modi's followers?

WHEN RAGA COURTED CONTROVERSY—RAHUL GANDHI'S FAMOUS TWEETS:

❖ 'If India is a computer, Congress is its default programme.'
❖ 'Politics is everywhere.. it is in your shirt.. in your pants.. you are carrying it everywhere, 70% of the country are youngsters,they need to be powered.'
❖ 'Dalit community "needs the escape velocity of Jupiter" to achieve success.'
❖ 'My opinion of the ordinance is that it is complete nonsense and that it should be torn up and thrown out.'
❖ 'People call us an elephant.. We are not an elephant.. we are a beehive.. it's funny but think about it. Which is more powerful? Elephant or a beehive?'[11]

REFERENCES

1. http://www.firstpost.com/politics/why-modi-succeeded-but-rahul-failed-in-attracting-young-india-1055125.html?utm_source=ref_article

2. https://Twitter.com/ajaymaken/status/390704673151131648

3. http://www.rediff.com/news/report/when-congress-outsourced-its-spokesperson/20140106.htm

4. http://www.dnaindia.com/analysis/standpoint-the-congress-and-social-media-1915507

5. http://timesofindia.indiatimes.com/tech/tech-news/internet/Rural-internet-users-to-rise-to-85-million-by-June-2014-IAMAI/articleshow/24541211.cms

6. PTI

7. http://blogs.reuters.com/india/2013/09/25/shashi-tharoor-on-congress-social-media-plans-digital-presence-of-gandhis/

8. http://indiatoday.intoday.in/story/rahul-gandhi-fiasco-times-now-interview-congress-media/1/342874.html

8. http://www.indiatvnews.com/print/news/digivijay-singh-congress-leader-who-loves-controve-11541-4.html

9. http://timesofindia.indiatimes.com/tech/social-media/Kapil-Sibal-debuts-on-Twitter-with-zero-following/articleshow/26527827.cms

10. http://timesofindia.indiatimes.com/india/AAP-effect-Govt-mulls-proposal-to-seek-public-view-before-framing-laws/articleshow/28518738.cms?utm_source=Twitter.com&utm_medium=referral&utm_campaign=timesofindia

11. http://www.firstpost.com/politics/from-beehive-to-jupiter-here-are-rahuls-quotable-quotes-1161705.html

8

AAP: Social Media Wonder?

There may be no way to measure the exact contribution of social media to politics, but the success story of the Aam Aadmi Party cannot be complete without social media driven by volunteers, multiplied with raw energy of youth, and fund raising via the web. Arvind Kejriwal and his mostly unknown team of hardworking and selfless professionals ensured that online posts turned into some votes. They made certain that of the people who were fired up with new ideas, debate, and desire to contribute to nation building—at least some actually stepped into poll booths. 'I think technology has been our saviour,' AAP's Somu Sundaram shares. 'Without social media, I believe we could not have reached out to these many people.'[1] The party's real success lies in getting its online team to 'act' offline. Ankit Lal, the party's social media incharge explains, 'Right from mobilizing people to sending across the correct information to people to countering the lies and confusion being spread by other parties, social media has proved to be an important tool.'

The AAP officially launched itself in November 2012 and has since fanned out in several different ways in the online world. The party has a website that is the central focus of its digital initiatives; from regular updates to funding details—

you can find everything on www.aamaadmiparty.org. Besides news updates and contributory blogs, the party has its presence on Facebook, Twitter, Google Plus, and YouTube. In their case, they have successfully used online and offline channels to feed into each other. AAP's identity was a tsunami of multiple ideas, approaches, and personalities that were brought to culmination—from the India Against Corruption campaign to a full-fledged political party with an agenda for the country.

The Delhi election in that sense was a gamechanger not just for the newcomer party but also a test for use of social media in politics. It was a matrix of whether or not social media and online campaigning plays a role in electoral success. 'While social media, on its own, cannot win elections, the outcome of the recent assembly elections and AAP's success in Delhi especially has shown that it can be a powerful influencer of votes, especially the swing voters or fence sitters,' asserts public relations honcho Dilip Cherian.

AAP has been a successful political story online. It has created, for example, a Facebook page for every single constituency in Delhi. Last month, the party did unexpectedly well in Delhi state elections, gaining dozens of seats and propelling Kejriwal to the position of Chief Minister. The AAP has strong support among Delhi's young and middle class—precisely the ones who are most active online.

It's fair to say that AAP's success lives irrespective of Kejriwal's short-lived stint at the job when he resigned from the Chief Minister's post on 14th February, 2014. He was unable to garner support for the anti-corruption Jan Lokpal bill and suffered a defeat in the assembly. Opposition politicians blocked the bill, which would have created an independent body with the power to investigate politicians and civil servants suspected of corruption. At the time this book went into print, Kejriwal was no longer the Chief Minister of Delhi.

But none of these controversies can take away the impact of the 'jadhu'. Of the three frontrunners in Delhi, the broom party has discernable virtual lead with more than 2,30,000 followers on Twitter, nearly neck to neck with BJP and leap years ahead of the Congress's 23,000 odd. This effective presence on one social media, was replicated through every platform that could feed the larger story of electoral success. So from Facebook, Twitter, Google Plus, Hangouts, blogs, its website and thousands of volunteers, AAP multiplied its presence across the board. Lal claimed that about 60,000 tweets were sent out with pro-AAP hashtags starting December 1, 2013, peaking on December 4 (voting day) with 24,000 tweets.

No one had anticipated that a one-year old party would either form the government or make a dent into the popularity of Congress or the BJP. What was also not expected was that social media would play a role in AAP's taking on Congress and BJP. During this election, Congress party led by the three time Chief Minister Sheila Dikshit, lost to Arvind Kejriwal by over 25,000 votes. Other national parties like BJP and Congress too have been expanding on social media but have often fallen short on counts of both numbers and energy. It would be naïve to ignore the contribution of the Internet in AAP's overall success matrix.

What clearly came across in AAP's use of social media is how they used it as a means and not as an end. As someone wittily put it, social media is an ingredient, not an entrée. This ingredient most definitely changed the outcome for AAP, amplified its message, and swelled its fan base and loyalty. According to the Twitter trends for a day before AAP's first

144 / SHAILI CHOPRA

election result in the Delhi elections, their hashtags #Vote4Aam Aadmi Party and #AAPS weeping Delhi trended consistently all day on both Delhi and India trends. Additionally, the social media team planned its online campaigning in such a way that the 48 hours to the final counting of votes brought it enormous audience through usage of special tools like news amplifying software and applications. For example, AAP claimed that they reached 3.5 million people just before voting day with an app called Thunderclap, a platform that's squarely focussed on augmenting campaigns. It is a platform that amplifies a discussion among some to many.[2]

Explaining Thunderclap, Lalsaid, 'We did a campaign on Thunderclap which did the trick for us. Thunderclap is a platform on which you can run campaigns. In this, people join a campaign through Facebook or Twitter and a Tweet or Facebook status goes out at the time the campaign matures.'[3] The website of Thunderclap showed that AAP's campaign matured at 4 pm on 2nd December and it had 10,151 campaigners with a total social media reach of 35,15,135 people. So the tweets and Facebook statuses went on walls of 10,151 people whose total social media reach was more than 3.5 million.[4]

AAP and social media have gone hand in hand through the inception of the party and its astonishing rise. In fact, this jugalbandi began even before the party was formed, in early 2013. As part of Anna Hazare's movement, Anna's most vocal and visible deputy, Arvind Kejriwal, set course to befriend social media. A former Indian Revenue Service officer, who had a pioneering role in constructing India's Right To Information (RTI) act, Arvind Kejriwal arrived on Facebook with a webpage called India Against Corruption to popularize the Jan Lokpal movement.

During this time, a young TV producer Abhinandan Sekri—in awe of Kerjiwal's work at NGO Parivatan, got latched on to the plans for India Against Corruption (IAC) under the Anna banner. Sekri used communication as the bedrock of the movement and included more and more people into it. This is when social media really became the nucleus of expansion. 'Initially we needed more people to join us and so we decided to use Facebook and Twitter to communicate with people who were becoming a part of it. For example, communicating a change in location for the meeting point or a protest, Jantar Mantar or Raj Ghat,' Sekri recalls. The IAC connect with social media in that sense happened more out of necessity, than as a well thought out strategy. It was cost-effective as the group was not flush with funds to spend to begin with. 'I remember when Anna was fasting at Jantar Mantar, we didn't have money to pay for the tent or *tamboo* for that day. We didn't have 3 lakhs in the account, and the tent was worth ₹5 lakh.' In dire circumstances, the group used the most basic ways to raise money. 'We just put a sheet on the ground and asked people to donate. We took initial money and ensured everyone got a receipt.' Having realized that money wasn't going to be easy to raise, not initially, IAC used a cost-effective outlet in social media. 'We figured the solution was to open all channels for volunteers, funding and donations and communication via the fastest viral mode, which was social media.'

However, once the differences between Anna Hazare and Kejriwal became apparent, the latter had to start from scratch for himself and for AAP.

'There were strong synergies in both but there were problems. Some moved on but a lot of people stayed with AAP since they believed in what we were doing,' shares

Ankur Srivastava, an engineer by profession but also a digital resource within AAP. 'So starting from scratch was the only way, but we had constant support and people came forward to help, which made our presence stronger both offline and online,' he added.[5]

One such party member was Pankaj Gupta who played a crucial part in the initial take-off for the party's funding. As a professional engineer, Gupta had worked for 25 years at various senior positions in software companies but he wanted to participate in politics and contribute through social work. He joined AAP and has been associated with the Jan Lokpal movement on a full time basis.

Gupta used his understanding of software models to plan AAP's fund-raising plan. It all culminated online. The party's website, started in January, launched a solid effort to raise money. It started with a lakh of rupees a day but that wasn't enough and so the party launched a digital campaign for donations.

DONATION DRIVE

By its own admission, AAP was attempting to change how political parties and elections work in India by introducing a more transparent style of functioning. On its website, it sought support so they could challenge the established political parties. 'We seek clean money from people like you, so that we can make a difference for you,' the website claims. It goes on to add, 'AAP will not put up any candidates with criminal backgrounds. It will also not put up more than one person from the same family.'

India has not had a history of transparency in election funding or declaration of party fund raising. Unlike in the United States where fund raising is a completely transparent process and there is accountability to the last dollar—in India, party donations are not talked about, any corporation or individual contributing to a political party is shrouded in controversy if such information is leaked out. AAP broke from traditional and sought to make public all its political fund raising. It made donations to the party public and open to scrutiny. Using the website for this went a long way in establishing transparency for seeking contributions, AAP created a first in recent electoral history.

Lal explains that new innovative ways worked for them because people expected them to be different. People bought the AAP story. They believe in getting more transparency. 'Being a new party, AAP had to resort to unconventional ways. As from our experience during the Lokpal movement, we were very well aware as well as well-versed on how to use social media for different purposes. Generating donations, using public inputs for the manifesto, keeping people informed about on ground events in Delhi, were some of the efforts,' says Lal.

Its website, very much a part of AAP's online activity, proved to be a launch pad for the party's overall existence. As donations started trickling in, the party began an e-mail drive to multiply the funding. 'The amount jumped to ₹3-4 lakh,' says Gupta in an interview to the *Indian Express*, 'still not enough'.

Short of three months to go for the Assembly polls, the fund-raising team decided that it was time to up the ante on fund raising as the election crescendo heightened. Gupta says in the *Express* interview, 'Meetings were held with business groups in several cities—Delhi, Mumbai, Bangalore, Gurgaon—where Kejriwal interacted with entrepreneurs. More than ₹25 lakh were raised in a single meeting. Around

150 people who attended the first few meetings would convince others to attend similar meetings.'

The party next put their cause to the Indian diaspora. 'We announced Google Hangout sessions with Kejriwal. Nearly ₹50 lakh were raised in one meeting,' Gupta adds.[6] Q&A sessions were held with Indians in the United States, Britain, Australia, Belgium, and Germany. This ensured the non-resident Indian was plugged into the politics beyond just the headlines. They even got NRIs to leave video messages of support on YouTube.[7]

AAP's website was direct and spelt its intentions right upfront. Those logging in were asked for donations and membership. This kept the focus in place and the website fairly simple. In United States, Barack Obama built upon his campaign on a concept that became famous as MyBO short for My.BarackObama.com. He empowered his supporters to host events and fund raisers on his behalf. In a simple but carefully constructed form, the website guided anyone willing to do an event to bring awareness to Obama's campaign. This was in addition to simply inviting people to donate for the campaign, which was a three-step procedure—Amount, Name, and Payment. Just streamlining his website and focusing on precisely what Obama and his team hoped to garner for it—money and database—built them an ocean of data that they could splice differently every single day.

The Observer analysed and compared Obama's online approach of 2008 to 'a multimedia company capable of competing with the traditional press in communicating with potential supporters. And that audience, in turn, has responded with hundreds of millions of dollars in campaign contributions, thousands and thousands of volunteer hours, and instant, on-demand outrage directed at media outlets whose coverage is deemed unfair to the candidate.'[8]

David Talbot for the *MIT Technology Review* summed it up, 'Obama, the former Chicago community organizer, created the ultimate online political machine.'

AAP by its own admission followed elements of the Obama strategy. The Obama campaign used the Internet to create a large volunteer base and reached out to every person to nudge them to vote for them. AAP too used social media to multiply and strengthen its volunteer base. Thereafter it was the many visits on its website to garner funds. A similar strategy to raise funds was originally adopted by the Barack Obama team in the run-up to 2008 when they targeted individual donors rather than public funds.

CROWDSOURCING MANIFESTO

In a bid to keep its manifesto open to the public, AAP crowd-sourced suggestions to build its party's agenda. The effort was unique, created a buzz, and got people thinking. It was an effort for people to engage and contribute in a way they hadn't before. For years, the government had been criticized for putting up policies that the people it targeted couldn't relate to. This effort to crowdsource was being touted as a way to reach out to more people, and put their problems in the forefront. Whether or not these crowdsourced solutions prove to work, the effort to build a manifesto in this matter is a departure from the past when select politicians announced a darbar and listed out a plan.

Part of its strategy was also to ensure they convert fencesitters among voters to the benefit of AAP. On social media, the key to gaining credibility was interaction and answering people's queries. When you engage with people and answer their queries, they get attached to your ideology and thus becomes part of the overall process. 'Twitter was the base platform for us for interacting with people followed by Facebook. Additionally, there were several ways in which we converted fencesitters. Arvind [Kejriwal], Manish [Sisodia], Yogendra [Yadav], etc had several rounds of meetings with such groups,' says Lal.

CLARITY IN COMMUNICATION

What such conversations helped with was the idea of consistent and clear communication. One of the stark differences between the social media strategy of Congress, BJP, and AAP is how AAP has ensured their communication does not get altered along the decentralized channel of the party's social media youngsters. Most of AAP's volunteers were well-known. And in some ways the handles on Twitter have been doing a consistent job. Sekri interprets the reasons for this relative social-media warmth towards AAP as 'something people are new to and a story that heralds change.' While there is no clear social media model, the highly decentralized approach of the party has actually helped it. 'Traditional parties have baggage of factionalism, and rumours about party members can spike on Twitter. Here you have a party, which is new with no party in-fighting.' So was it that social media was more accommodating towards the newcomer? For one, the venom against existing policies and politicians was at an all time high and so anyone who offered change brought in a new and fresh thinking. 'It was this philosophical sense of governance that allow AAP due credibility online,' Sekri asserts.

There were thousands of cynics online but the social media messages was so focused that somewhere trolls were limited by the kind of communication adopted by AAP. Lal explains, 'Trolls are limited to a certain right wing faction of the Indian social media and they are so because they have been trained and instructed to be so. In our case we were very clear from day 1 that we should not behave that way. Our leaders conducted themselves in a very dignified way on social media, attacking only when equipped with substantial data to back their claims. This percolated to the volunteers as well.'

Lal says that they preferred to keep the flow of news limited to official handles on social media and insists that the messaging was always very dignified and never slanderous. 'All this can be attributed to success in maintaining decorum among AAP volunteers on social media.' The party's main face Kejriwal was tweeting for himself, there were clear mentions of the volunteers, discussions were launched, and a coordination group for its activists was formed as @AAPActivists.

MOBILIZING PEOPLE, SIMPLIFYING THE STRUCTURE

- ❖ Identify campaign
- ❖ Plan and decentralize
- ❖ Launch banner design
- ❖ Work on arrangement of Live telecast
- ❖ Posting of banner on Social media along with link of live telecast to drive people to a destination
- ❖ Decide if a Twitter trend is to be done. If yes, then hashtag planning, day and time of trend is worked upon
- ❖ At the specified time the team (and volunteers) comes online and tweets with the decided tag

ENGAGING AND RECOGNIZING THEIR VOTER

AAP's distinction also comes, in a subtle way, in the way they share stories of people online. The Congress and BJP's websites—aicc.org.in and BJP.org—are both informative, give out details about their members, list their icons from Gandhi to Vajpayee, but they fail to engage. On the AAP website, the motive and engagement is direct. It is immediately clear that they are looking for your support, money, time, and voluntary service. The argument that AAP needs to take to these measures because it is a fledgling party is invalid. In Obama's case, even now as he is President for second term, donations form a very integral part of the online strategy. Donations do not end with just the donor giving an amount to the party. Donations encourage engagement. They connect the candidate to the contributor. The Indian Congress has a button called 'Support the Congress' but it's formatted like filling a form on just about any website. It's also a poor effort in collating data of potential supporters, something AAP has done tremendously well by documenting those who are connecting on their site, seeking granular information of them, and then using it to their party's favour for the elections.

In a bid to stay connected with supporters, the party constantly kept in touch on social media channels like Facebook. A post a few days after the Delhi elections said, 'This whole movement was driven by your money. We estimated that we will need ₹20 crore to fight elections and you donated 20 crores. 20 crores of white money to fight a clean election. For the first time in Indian political history, a party stopped taking donation after it reached its target.'

While there is always need for information on past achievements, history, iconic members, and so on—the new online subscriber is edgy and wants to read and absorb recent events and data. By overloading their websites with history of nationalism for BJP or past speeches of Rahul Gandhi—the online teams of these mainstream parties reflect lethargy in understanding what occupies the minds of the people. These sites pale in comparison to AAP—which gives out its hash tag right on top—as their websites do not link to their social media at all. Narendra Modi is an exeption here, as his website is very social media friendly—every single sentence on his site can be tweeted as is. Twelve social media icons prompt you to share what you are reading through a constant bar on his site.

Another hook which garners support for AAP is the highlighted stories of those who have helped AAP. Their website carries numerous stories like these, which reflect on the dedication of various people from within India and overseas who are either supporting through fund raising or working pro bono. 'Senior lawyer, Dr Sanjay K. Paliwal has come from North Carolina to support AAP. He specially came from USA to support the cause. He is here to support Legal Cell. He has taken responsibility of New Delhi Lok Sabha Areas plus all other legal supporting needs if in other areas as well. He left all his other works and functioning for supporting the cause.' There are numerous such examples of people who travelled from overseas and took a sabbatical to help AAP.

LOW ON COST, HIGH ON PASSION

Passion, they say, is the gasoline of social media. By its own admission, AAP believes that the best thing about social media is the minimum cost involved. Put low cost and passion together and the party had a winner at hand. For Aam Aadmi Party, volunteers maintained party's social media pages free of cost. The party ideologies were shared to individuals through social media, and then passed on to friends, followers, groups, and pages so as to multiply effect. 'There is a very important message for people, and that is you do not need much money and other resources to win elections. That's the lesson at least I got from the Aam Aadmi Party victory,' shares India's IT czar N.R. Narayana Murthy.[9]

Additionally the party came into focus primarily for the way it used online platforms to mobilize crowds offline. Aam Aami Party arranged their meetings, protests and agendas through Facebook, Twitter, websites, and blogs. Whether to meet at India Gate or Jantar Mantar, where the protest would start and end—all information was primarily conveyed through social networks. 'Many political parties disagree that social media will be a decisive factor in the upcoming election but these parties are trying their best to woo the individuals engaged in social networks,' explains an article on Arvind Kejriwal's own website.[10]

In the wake of the state elections, as the countdown began, the party used a combination of awareness tools that amalgamated mobilizing, informing, and engaging online and through physical drives to create a buzz. The party called these volunteers the 'buzz team', which fanned out to the streets with a visibility campaign. The AAP volunteers distributed posters, caps, leaflets, and reminded the potential voter who AAP was and what it stood for. Their symbol of the jhadu (broom)—meant to reflect a clean-up of the political system—became a key catchword of this buzz campaign.

While the party employed digital media very effectively, a traditional symbol like the 'Gandhi topi' which stands for an old world value—social change—worked very well too. Lloyd Mathias, senior marketer and Director, GreenBean Ventures, explains the three features that set AAP's campaign apart. 'The sharp symbolism of the Gandhi topi and the jhadu.Two, the younger, non-political candidates representing the real aam aadmi. And three, reinforcing their commitment to nominating candidates with integrity by cancelling the nomination of a candidate who was found to be inappropriate.'[11]

AAP's sudden rise, popularity, and campaign hysteria even caught the attention of Nobel Laureate Amartya Sen. 'What Kejriwal has brought to the table is that if one has a few powerful messages, you can win elections with very little money. You can get a party ready fairly quickly to have a stunning debut. He has also given hope and confidence to a lot of people across various cities of the country to say we too can participate in the political process,' he said in an interview to NDTV.[12]

One wonders with this kind of success—a promising combination of online and offline power—what is it that brands can learn from India's most prolific political start-up? In a discussion with Exchange For Media, Shubhangi Agrawal of Troika Consulting lists down the following points:[13]

What can brands learn from AAP?

- **Competitor has strength? Negate it by making it your point of parity**

  Make your competitors differentiating factors your points of parity. Just like AAP built a plan around socio-economic policy and campaigned for its cause, the basic every party needs to do.

  More so AAP also spread awareness on its manifesto by popular hashtags such as—#AAP4WomenSafety,

#AAP4Swaraj, #AAP4Janlokpal and #AAPVision. These were accompanied by videos, interesting graphics, statistics, and interviews shared as updates on AAP's profiles.

- **Choose a compelling point of difference that the customer values**

Analyse gaps, look for consumer motivations, and frame your point of differentiation. The biggest issue around politics today is corruption and AAP surely captured it. AAP was also different in its communication strategy—it capitalized the power of social media and revived door-to-door campaigning. At a time when established parties were majorly glued to old-traditional methods, AAP was busy building its presence on social media.

- **Now is the era of ad-free branding! Don't get limited by advertising budgets**

Even with small advertising budget, the impact can be huge. You just need to integrate strategy with creativity and develop an innovative communication plan. In the current age of social media, at least the youth is just a click away!

According to recent statistics by Socialbakers (dated 17th December, 2013):

* The fan growth of AAP's Facebook page is remarkable with an average increase of 1,16,310 fans per week. For BJP this number is 40,582, only 35 percent of AAP's figure.

* In a very short span of time, the followers of Arvind Kejriwal on Twitter are growing at 50,236 per week approximately the same rate as that of Narendra Modi at 47,507 per week.

* AAP was also able to gather support from Indians based outside such as US, UK, UAE, Turkey etc.

- **Customer is the new God**

Brands now revolve around consumers. With the current market clutter, the power has shifted from brands to the customers. Both the identity and promise of AAP revolve around the common man.

AAP was able to spread its aam-aadmi centric promises effectively via social media. While a very significant social media presence may not entirely get converted into votes, it's essential to create a buzz. It's a tendency of people to follow in tribes. AAP specifically targeted the new voters.

- **Customer engagement is now a two-way process**

Consumer engagement is the key to success. AAP was able to get a never before seen strength of motivated volunteers who campaigned its cause and became brand advocates.

AAP brought a new concept called 'Volunteering' in the election process. This term has always been associated with noble causes such as volunteering for NGOs etc. This way AAP was able to spread a very positive message and also engage common people.

- **To be... rather than to seem to be!**

Build your brand inside-out. AAP was the first party to publish an audited report of donations and expenses. It ensured its candidates had a clear background. And it clearly mentions that the parties motivations are not big government flats, extensive security etc. Its foundation is built on transparency which resonates with its corruption-free image outside.

Here social media and their websites have played an important role.

- **Small brands don't scare you?**

  Never underestimate a new entrant, a mistake BJP and Congress made this time. This is clearly evident from the election results and the above analysis.

SELF-CRITICAL, OPEN TO IDEAS?

In a section titled 'Your questions about AAP', the party took on the sceptics and the fencesitters head on. It picked up the most controversial questions floating in the media and social media against the party and raised it on its own website. 'Is AAP a B-team of the BJP or Congress?' or 'Is AAP not registered with election commission?' In an FAQ-style, but more in your face, the questions are then answered with clarification by AAP decimating the 'buzz' around its work or existence. It's a clever move and one that brought it admiration.

The party also used tele-tactics (recorded voice messages) to pump up the effort in reaching out to more people during the Delhi elections. A call from Arvind Kejrival, (recorded) '*Main Arvind Kejriwal bol raha hun*,' added to the communication armoury at AAP's disposal. The message, a promise of improved governance over other parties, would pose questions and answers to educate the person on the other side of the phone. Among many messages, here is an example of one where Kejriwal says, 'I was part of movements against corruption, protested against corruption, and faced police lathis. Then in March this year I was on fast for fifteen days against inflated water and electricity bills. If I had to become corrupt then I would have become a millionaire during service days,' he declares making a pitch for honesty. While for some such calls were a nuisance, there is no doubt it added to the brand recall of AAP. They also ensured that they put their message across in their own tone and voice, in the most literal sense.

AAP's researcher Vinay Kumar Mittal in an interview to *Deccan Herald* explains the rationale behind the campaign, 'We have always been looking out for innovative and low-cost methods to reach out to people. Through this, we intend to reach out to people personally who are away from the ambit of our social media campaigns.'[14]

There is little doubt that the Aam Admi Party has benefited from the relentless media exposure. Rajdeep Sardesai, the Editor-in-chief of CNN-IBN credited Kejriwal's use of media power as one of the lessons Rahul Gandhi could learn. 'If Rahul has "Ma" (mother) by his side, Kejriwal has the 'media'. It is to the credit of the ever accessible Kejriwal and his team that they used every communication weapon—Facebook, Twitter, television—to create a larger than life image for the party. By contrast, Rahul has remained imprisoned behind the forbidding gates of Lutyens Delhi, not giving a single proper interview, refusing to take hard questions, staying away from the social media.'[15]

THE WIN, THE FALL

Arvind Kejriwal did become the Chief Minister of India's most powerful state, the capital Delhi. One would have to acknowledge that social media contributed to his rise, in bringing awareness about AAP and casting the net wide in India and overseas to raise money and garner support. Kejriwal became CM even though BJP won more seats—but didn't have majority. Kejriwal had announced that in the cause of a hung election in Delhi, his party would not take the support of either the BJP or Congress to form government. But on pressure from all quarters, AAP went to the extent of asking an open question on their site and their social media 'Should AAP form the government?' in a bid to get the 'individual voice' included in government formation. Eventually with Congress' support, AAP's Kejriwal was appointed CM.

THE CONTROVERSIES

Kejriwal's stint in the Delhi government lasted 49 days and what brought him down was the Jan LokPal bill. The anti-corruption bill was blocked in the state assembly and this was a blow to AAP and Kejriwal who came to power on the anti-corruption plank.

Kejriwal's 49 days were under the spotlight and not bereft of its lows. AAP's massive online fan base that had once praised them also criticized them. For example when Kejriwal held a dharna and slept two nights on the streets in the cold as a mark of protest to get more control of the police force, he was criticized for using ways that might appear unconstitutional or unbecoming of a Chief Minister. Worse, his party's protest led to closing of metro stations, bringing normal life to standstill, earning him flak. Suddenly the same Twitter world that hailed him as a hero, mocked him with hashtags like #AAPDrama #YoKejriwalSoBrave. He was criticized for not maturing into a politician after a solid performance in Delhi elections. BBC's Andrew North pointed out in his piece, 'He never really stopped being a protestor and never looked comfortable as a politician.'

This was the same party that had proved politicians have suddenly found the value of interacting with the common man over Facebook and Twitter, helpfully answering questions and taking feedback.

AAP has no doubt been an online success but that's when the troubles begin to surface as more and more attention is on their social-cast or broadcast. Having reached this stage, the question for AAP is, what next? The challenge is to bring more digital experts who can bring foresight and start work in advance on new platforms and apps that can come in handy in augmenting electioneering in the years ahead. AAP's birth, political career has milestones in social media. For them the challenge has been to convert this popularity into governance—something substantial, long-term, and more interactive

The material challenge that they will face is how to replicate the success in an urban city where most people are on handphones and Internet to a larger electoral base. Can the story of an urban centre and its social media reach, spin a bigger story for AAP? It's here that the party will need to sew in more ideas on offline outreach of its online presence. And in that sense it may need to reinvent its positioning. 'Sure enough, there is a lot of handwork for them if they have to spin this out of Delhi and take it across. Finding the right people, committed, faultless people etc. isn't easy. But I suppose people would take their Delhi show as something that can be duplicated across the country,' shares Prathap Suthan, managing partner, Bang in the Middle in an interview with MXM India.[16]

Another relevant question around social media remains the issue of how such data collection, user engagement is being put to use. In Obama's case splicing the data according to demographics, identifying fencesitters, and later turning energies towards it helped him garner support. AAP's Lal admits there is much data available to plug in the social media piece in India's case. 'Analytics are there but plugging this data to electoral data is not possible. We are not engaging any companies for this. The team is competent enough and as per our experience, normal marketing strategies do not work for us so engaging mainstream companies is not useful for us.' Going forward it remains to be seen how different data firms put together a powerful combination of tools that make the task of campaign managers far more focused than their current obsession with buzz created by social media.

Social supremacy might not be enough to win votes in a country where a large number of the voting population lies outside of the pool but having an influential voice out there is near mandatory. 'While we in no way endorse any political parties, or any such social agenda, the AAP campaign showed that there is more to elections than just promotional smartphones, cheesy anthems, and jarring songs,' says Kamakshi S. of Techtree[17]. If social media is an extension of real policies and plans, then it can change fortunes for people and parties. 'Social media is an extension of human beings online. And Kejriwal knew this,' says Sekri. 'He used it as a basic element of people to people communication. He played an all or nothing game—raised his stakes—his popularity has a lot to do with this art of betting the bank. I think people found an outlet in social media and appreciated such risk-taking to change the country's corruption fabric,' he explains.

It's difficult to ignore how effectively AAP married its strategies for online communication and physical mobiliza-tion. Every effort was made to rouse the youth and change was promised. The story presented and packaged in its most basic elements, the broom vroom, the perspective of simplicity in its manifesto, and importantly the pitch that there would be more power to the people—have all contributed to scripting the success of AAP.

REFERENCES

1. http://www.aamaadmiparty.org/page/truth-vs-hype-trending-democracy

2. https://www.thunderclap.it/en/projects/6584-click-for-india

3. http://www.firstpost.com/politics/delhi-polls-aap-leads-on-Twitter-facebook-but-is-it-enough-1264229.html

4. https://www.thunderclap.it/en/projects/6584-click-for-india

5. http://lighthouseinsights.quora.com/The-Organic-Growth-Story-Of-Aam-Aadmi-Party-AAP-On-Social-Media

6. http://www.indianexpress.com/news/meet-kejriwals-friends-who-were-behind-success-of-aam-aadmi-party/1207728/0

7. http://www.youtube.com/watch?v=24mkKV1El10 and http://www.youtube.com/watch?v=v1HhQA3XMfI

8. http://observer.com/2008/07/power-of-mybo-obamas-web-site-surmounts-news/?show=all

9. Arvind Kejriwal has redefined what is possible, says Narayana Murthy—Article by Karthik Subbaraman & Indu Nandakumar, *Economic Times,* December 12, 2013.

11. In an interview with the author.

12. http://www.indianexpress.com/news/aaps-rise-has-challenged-established-institutions-amartya-sen/1207656/

13. In an interview with the author

14. http://www.deccanherald.com/content/359557/hello-aam-aadmi-calling.html)sept

15. http://ibnlive.in.com/blogs/rajdeepsardesai/1/64985/arvind-kejriwalaap-success-has-many-lessons-for-rahul-gandhi.html

16. http://www.mxmindia.com/2013/12/the-making-of-brand-aam-aadmi-party/

17. http://www.techtree.com/content/features/5159/social-media-shape-successful-election-campaigns-india.html

9

Other Political Parties and Social Media

We have, in the previous chapters, looked at the social media strategies of major parties and their spearheads. Though most of the limelight is hogged by the BJP and the AAP in the social media space, other regional parties have also made an attempt to use online and social media to propagate their parties' message. The next generation of leaders, party's official outfits, and volunteers are all logging on to where the virtual drama unfolds. Some have continued this experiment with gusto and others have abandoned the ship half way. Lalu Prasad Yadav is among the latest to embrace the Internet.

RJD'S LALU FALLS FOR SOCIAL MEDIA

Lalu Yadav made his debut on Twitter with a philosophical message. 'Only change is constant. With change, we change, finally on Twitter,' said the first tweet of the Rashtriya Janata Dal (RJD) chief on his account, @laluprasadrjd.

His entry, just a few months before elections, goes on to prove how politicians are realizing the importance of staying in touch with voters through their preferred media. After seeing mainstream parties garner massive support online, other parties are making an attempt to catch up.

'Let us all work together towards a common goal for better future,' said another tweet by Lalu. PTI in a report highlighted that Prasad's entry in the social media has been radical, considering his comment 'Ye IT YT kya hota hai' (what is this IT etc).[1] His Twitter account garnered over 15,000 followers within a few weeks of his joining the microblogging site.

TRINAMOOL CONGRESS

Mamata Banerjee has a verified Facebook account with over 6,00,000 fans and it is regularly updated with news, pictures, and stories about the party. 'We should raise our voices and stand by principles—conviction, values, and integrity,' says Mamata Banerjee on Facebook.[2] The Trinamool website says prominently, 'If you are a regular visitor on the social-networking-site "Facebook" then you must have noticed that Trinamool Congress Chairperson and West Bengal Chief Minister Ms Mamata Banerjee is the newest high-value member on Facebook.' It further adds that Trinamool Congress' Chairperson and West Bengal Chief Minister's decision to join Facebook comes at a time when there is immense demand to know about what Banerjee's thought process is. The website makes no qualms about the fact that TMC's social media push is an exercise to defend mainstream media's coverage of Banerjee. 'The presence on Facebook comes at such a time when certain media organizations were indulging in concocted stories against Ms Banerjee, the entire game was so well-planned and well-orchestrated that some section of the opposition party took refuge of Facebook to malign her image by putting up cartoons and "morphed" pictures.'

That social media too has its challenges given the openness it encourages, TMC party spokesperson Derek O' Brien in a more frank debate did share that there are challenges of the medium as well. In an NDTV show he shared, 'People think you can have instant solutions to the problems of West Bengal on Twitter. Act now or else...'

BIJU JANATA DAL (BJD)

In mid-2013, Odisha Chief Minister Naveen Patnaik inaugurated the official website for BJP and encouraged party workers to use social media to woo young voters. He said over 40 percent of the total electorate in the state comprised the youth. 'The new generation is using social media, which is a powerful media for youth communication programmes. We need to be engaged in the social media to communicate with the youth,' Patnaik said after inaugurating the party website.[3] Later in October 2013, the BJD Twitter account was launched. Its Facebook account, though unverified, has just about 5000 likes.

JANATA DAL

Nitish Kumar is on Facebook with a fan page that boasts over 25,000 fans but his Twitter account has been slow to pick up. He hasn't tweeted since July 2012. Further he made headlines for criticizing Modi's use of social media in politics in 2013 when he was quoted saying, 'When famous economist Amartya Sen praised the Bihar model of development, divisive forces hailing from a party led a campaign on social media to assassinate his character...their intolerance towards things they do not like reminds me of the days of Emergency in 1975 when freedom of speech was throttled.' Kumar was taking a dig at Modi who has over 3 million followers on Twitter and this comment was made after Janata Dal broke off its alliance with BJP.

The more active social media politician in JD is Deputy Chief Minister of Bihar, Sushil Kumar Modi who has also pumped up his presence on social media. The Deputy Chief Minister has presence on Facebook, Twitter, and YouTube.

AIADMK AND JAYALALITHAA

Ruling AIADMK in Tamil Nadu put its various tech wings to work for polls with a special thrust on wooing young voters. This strategy involved using social media and IT power as it gears for the 2014 Lok Sabha polls, all with the ambition of strengthening the position of supremo Jayalalithaa. A report filed by PTI said that the party is targeting the first-time voters as being done by parties such as BJP which is harping on its 'Modi youth connect'. AIADMK's youth outfits—student and youth wings—are all set to reach out to the young electorate by launching a campaign through SMS.[4] The party is present on Facebook with Jayalalithaa's unofficial page with about 30,000 fans.

DRAVIDA MUNNETRA KAZHAGAM AND KARUNANIDHI

Karunanidhi made his debut on Twitter and Facebook in 2013, and is very keen about the response he gets on the social media. He personally reviews the responses every two days and encourages his account managers to report to him about criticisms made by his followers on social media. His website www.kalaignarkarunanidhi.com is up to speed with news flow and keeps users up to date on social media updates, blogs, and speeches. In fact, the DMK chief's Facebook account has over 1,00,000 likes. There are close to 19,000 followers on his Twitter handle @kalaignar89. Clearly, having the entire Sun TV media network as a part of the family business, Karunanidhi's website is big on mobile apps and video. It runs its own video channel and uploads new clips regularly.

COMMUNIST PARTY OF INDIA (MARXIST) STAYS OFF

Left parties, owing to their stand on globalization, technology, and social media have kept an arm's distance from networking sites. Prakash Karat and his contemporaries have not taken to social media in any official capacity. 'We acknowledge that social media has a tremendous reach. Our website provides the latest content. We do have plans to expand in social media before the elections and rope in more operators,' says CPI(M) central committee member Nilotpal Basu in an article in *Hindustan Times*.[5]

OTHERS

Over the last 18 months, regional parties of Karnataka, Maharashtra, and Bihar have joined the party on the social networks. Nationalist Congress Party, Maharashtra Navnirman Sena (MNS), and Shiv Sena, are all now on social media. In Bihar, Lok Janshakti Party (LJP) President Ramvilas Paswan also joined social media to woo the youth. Lighthouse Insights shares that some of these 'did spike up their activity on social media but the move lacked the intent and objective.'[6] For example, in early 2013, the Karnataka Pradesh Congress launched a big drive online when KPCC president G. Parameshwara interacted with netizens on Google Hangout. He also launched the party's Twitter, Facebook, and YouTube accounts and released its audio-video publicity material. The party promised to update netizens through these media on a daily basis. In an interview with the *Times of India*, Parameshwara said this was an attempt to 'keep pace with the modern world. There are many educated and ambitious youth on social media—it's their platform. We're here to develop the link with them and address their aspirations.' He said the target audience was youth and women as they have the power to correct the system.

In Maharashtra, Shiv Sena, NCP, and MNS have launched their websites and increased reach through Facebook and Twitter. In an interview to *Economic Times,* Nawab Malik, Chief Spokesperson of State NCP said, 'We have realized that it's very important to reach out to urban voters, especially the middle and higher middle classes, who are vocal about various issues. We decided that the best way to do this is by using non-traditional media. Apart from this, we are also aware of the role of radio and regional television.'[7]

At the Indian National Lok Dal, Ajay Chautala's sons— Dushyant and Digvijay—launched a special campaign to win over the youth of Haryana by their planned foray into social media. Hindustan Times reported that Gen-Next of Chautalas had virtually taken over the reins of INLD and hoped to win over the youth of Haryana with a major push on social media.[8] The initiative however lacked the punch on social. The report said they maintain a 'war room' in Gurgaon where all electoral strategies are being drawn up.

Lighthouse Insights puts out some challenges among social media strategies of regional parties.[9]

1. The social media presence created by most of the politicians is inactive among regional parties. Best example is the presence of the Chief Minister of that state on social media and often they are inactive.

2. Creating a presence and showing intent to inform as well as engage are two different things. The political parties have understood the step one but not the later.

3. Zero integration between websites and social presence. The websites should at least list the official social networks of the politicians or their respective parties.

REFERENCES

1. http://www.thehindu.com/news/national/now-lalu-prasad-is-on-Twitter/article5580812.ece

2. https://aitmc.org/features.php?latid=103

3. http://www.odishareporter.in/top_news/naveen-inaugurates-bjds-website

4. http://articles.economictimes.indiatimes.com/2013-09-29/news/42503138_1_youth-wing-aiadmk-tamil-nadu

5. http://www.hindustantimes.com/specials/coverage/myindia-myvote/chunk-ht-ui-myindiamyvote-leadingstories/a-political-trend-regional-parties-try-out-social-media/sp-article10-1141338.aspx

6. http://www.hindustantimes.com/specials/coverage/myindia-myvote/chunk-ht-ui-myindiamyvote-

leadingstories/a-political-trend-regional-parties-try-out-social-media/sp-article10-1141338.aspx

7. http://articles.economictimes.indiatimes.com/2013-03-28/news/38099816_1_ncp-and-mns-social-media-state-ncp

8. http://www.hindustantimes.com/India-news/NewDelhi/Young-Chautalas-plan-party-makeover-eye-social-media/Article1-1032786.aspx

9. http://lighthouseinsights.in/political-parties-of-bihar-are-logging-onto-social-media-but-is-it-effective.html

10

Social Media in 2014 General Elections

A political party or a politician trends on social media nearly every day. The upcoming elections in 2014 have kept politics and leaders on their toes and making news. The Delhi elections of 2013 and the upsurge of the AAP in popularity charts validated the significant role social media plays in spreading information and influencing the final outcome. For the first time, a one-year-old party—grown substantially by campaigns on social media—established the government in the national capital. This outcome also suggested that India's middle-class and Internet-savvy population were clued into politics and helped tilt the results in favour of AAP. A study by Bangalore-based Simplify-360 found that 31 percent of Twitter users in India actually read a tweet on politics. The report also showed there was a five-fold increase in buzz in social media for Kejriwal after Delhi election win. It further suggested there is presence of 24 percent of Indian voters on social media which is a key factor in determining the poll results because 2.6 crore Indians read tweets related to elections.[1]

Indian politicians such as Narendra Modi, Arvind Kejriwal, Shashi Tharoor and others have invested significantly in social media. Now all of them are squarely focused on using these as a key message-medium for elections.

Bhupendra Khanal from Simplify-360, in an interview with the author, says, 'We expect all political parties and politicians to use the media and take maximum benefit out of it. The trend is already seen in most cases. Huge numbers of voters are participating in discussion in social channels, while impact may be bigger than this number as this population can influence votes of their families too. We expect at least 20 percent vote swing through Social Media in 2014.'

The Economic Times analysed two sets of data—search volumes from Google Trends and proprietary data from social media analytics firm Simplify-360—to report that Kejriwal has dominated the digital discourse since the first week of December, when results of assembly elections in Delhi and four other states were declared.[2] The data, the report said, confirms what people have been observing anecdotally on social media for weeks—the growing online popularity of AAP. It further added that AAP had succeeded in relegating the buzz about Modi to the background, despite the well-crafted strategy and considerable resources his supporters pump into the effort. At the time the book went to print, Kejriwal had resigned—something that began to impact his overall popularity factor online.

Undoubtedly, social media has given a voice to the common people. Pundits, analysts, party spokespersons are featured on news channels every night to put across their views and justify the stand of their respective parties. Additionally, news channels often pick stories that broke on social media. All these factors make it central to news flow these days. Major political episodes in the country become trending topics and all sides are able to make TV news headlines quite regularly.

Since social media has also become a via-media to put news, views, and opinion on mainstream media—its effectiveness multiplies and makes social media important to election 2014.

A report by IAMAI and IRIS Knowledge Foundation shows that of India's 543 constituencies, 160 can be termed as 'high impact'—that is, they will most likely be influenced by social media in the next general elections. 'In today's India, the number of social media users to achieve this end has reached a tipping point. May be not in every one of the 543 constituencies but certainly in a significant number of them to warrant the conclusion that they have the power to influence elections and therefore government formation.' As the report explains, high impact constituencies are those where the numbers of Facebook users are more than the margin of victory of the winner in the last Lok Sabha election, or where Facebook users account for over 10 percent of the voting population. The study then goes on to declare 67 constituencies as medium-impact, 60 as low-impact, and 256 as no-impact constituencies.[3]

Social media has gone beyond just being a fight between people with different views to something more substantial. It has encompassed parties and politicians. The heightened interest in politics of those on Twitter led to massive attention to details by political parties on social media strategies. Rallies are getting live-tweeted and social media has become the primary source of information. Many programmes are live streamed on YouTube and politicians are conducting Google Hangouts to discuss strategies with NRIs and other political and business constituents. The expanding middle-class and web-savvy population sees online an extension of their candidates. Meena Yadav, a homemaker shares that social media is an extension of any political candidate. More importantly, they feel that they finally have access to information about their political figures and leaders. Talking of Modi, Meena shares 'we can hear him speak anywhere in the country and can relate to different issues. I feel connected to him as I think he's a strong man capable of taking very strong decisions and that's what our country needs right now.' Rajesh Lalwani of Blogworks admits such interest within the public at large in politics and society has forced more and more leaders to embrace the Internet and accept its social norms. However, he warns, politicians eyeing 2014 must be watchful of how they plan to use social media so that it doesn't backfire. 'It is not about the sudden rush; it's that the sudden rush has not been thought through by most people. It's not about creating fake accounts and getting fans. It is about what we have spoken earlier to say why one is using this medium— the sense of purpose, engagement, and transparency that leaders wish to bring about.'

There are several candidates using social media. Narendra Modi is banking on India272.com and NitiCentral and others to drive his campaign forward, backed by his own website NarendraModi.in. Additionally, Modi ensures the hashtags are well publicized through Twitter and Facebook pages to ensure his different speeches are made to trend. A combination of cartoons, infographics, and punch-laden tweets are planned in the run-up to the campaign. Arvind Kejriwal (while Delhi Chief Minister and even as he was dethroned) campaigned on social media and answered media queries to justify his comments and decisions. His popularity had been pitched right against Modi's as the PM candidate from Congress—not officially announced—is absent from social media. However Congress' catch up and Rahul Gandhi's new media blitzkrieg includes a dedicated budget and plan for social media through the Congress handle and that of its spokespersons.

Among the many other candidates is Nandan Nilekani, who is standing from Bangalore, and social media and digital strategies are core to his campaign. The co-founder of Infosys Technologies is putting all technology to use according to a report by *India Today*. 'Besides utilizing public forums that are usually dominated by seasoned politicians, maximizing the use of social/ digital media and engaging people with fresh ideas are other objectives of the methodology. With the launch of social/ digital media blitzkrieg in favour of Nilekani, the campaign will aim at capturing issues plaguing the city, and will have an interactive and participatory approach to ensure that more number of people (voters) are involved in it, according to sources.'[4]

Meera Sanyal, who stood as an Independent in the 2009 elections and later joined AAP from Mumbai, admits that social media is influencing voters. 'I believe so—especially in the group of voters below 25.' As someone active on Twitter, she feels, 'It is making it possible for the people to make their voice heard in real time. It is also a great equalizer—the barriers to sharing one's opinions and being heard by large numbers of people are now lower than ever before.'

Rajesh Lalwani adds that social media 'has also become important as the patterns of usage of the social medium by political parties and leaders are evolving. They are starting to understand the nature and value of this phenomenon better in terms of ability to engage citizens through conversations and the value of data that social conversations throw up. These help decipher mood, emerging and shifting themes, role of technology in scaling up, micro-targeting and so on.'

It's hard to finitely deduce that social media led to higher voter turnout or a stronger verdict but the final analysis of elections in India is unlikely to be complete without social media pitching in. The year 2013 has shown, anecdotally and with analysis, that indeed AAP managed to muster deep engagement and involvement in the political arena. Our leaders mustn't forget—if a large chunk of their voters are in rural India ploughing fields—a good measure of their voters are also sowing political seeds in social media. A computer screen may not be an electronic voting machine but it's an indispensable tool in this age in urging people to eventually head there.

5 Reasons Why Social Media Matters For 2014

- Wide reach
- Cost-effective
- Easy to implement
- Specific returns on investment—ability to track number of people it touches, engages with
- Direct communication between voter, potential voter, and leaders

2014: POLITICIANS WOO SOCIAL MEDIA

Rajesh Lalwani, of Blogworks has asked on three questions every candidate should look to answer before putting out a social strategy

1. Character—'Who am I'
2. Stickiness—'Why should people consume my message and keep coming back'
3. Shareability—'Why will people engage with my content and share'

References

1. http://www.socialsamosa.com/2014/01/election-analysis-simplify-indian-election-2014/

2. http://articles.economictimes.indiatimes.com/2014-01-17/news/46301596_1_narendra-modi-arvind-kejriwal-assembly-elections

3. http://www.esocialsciences.org/General/A2013412184534_19.pdf

4. http://indiatoday.intoday.in/story/infosys-co-founder-nandan-nilekani-launches-op-agile-to-win-polls/1/336305.html

11

Is Social Media Indicative of Social Churn in India?

Is our expression an extension of us? Are we the same people on Facebook and Twitter as in flesh and blood? Is our hunger for instant gratification, communication, and expression just signs of our own impatience or perhaps a fundamental change in the way we as humans think and operate? Express and opine. Meet and greet. How are we beyond social networkers, the new beasts of society? Are we the harbingers of a new social change as expressed by the acerbic prompting we now engage in? Are all Indians deep within some sort of political animals? The surge in social networking has been manifested in display of 'both frustration and celebration on online platforms,' says Nandana Sengupta who is a doctoral candidate in Economics at Carnegie Mellon University. There is a new need among people to post or tweet as they think. Ever so often the enthusiasm of political awareness and un-derstanding (or semi-understanding) is reflected in instant opinions, pins, and timelines. 'I think the share and retweet buttons have altered us as a society. From being inner directed, we have become outer directed. From being evasive, to being invasive.

From being faceless to having a voice. We have changed from being subjugated to standing up. For instance, today, a man in Meerut can stand up and criticize a minister openly,' shares Swapan Seth of Equus Advertising and an advisor to several brands. Media watcher and owner Anurag Batra agrees but also warns of the downsides of so many opinions. 'Internet is the great equalizer. It is the medium that allows everyone to post their comment in the cyberspace, regardless of creed, social position, or gender. Everyone is allowed an opinion, and the internet keeps a record of every opinion that has ever been shared on it. This, however, poses a problem, where all opinions posted are less-than-sterling.'[1]

Seth's argument does point to the hypersensitivity of our fingertips and how quickly they can 'speak'—even before thinking, as it is in some cases. This constant desire to share extends to the extreme, aggressive, and vitriolic content that floods social networking sites. There is also an impulsive desire to participate in political discussions, campaigns, and movements—something that was conspicuous by its absence in India and Indians in the last two decades. So after the era of real revolutions and wars, piped up protests and freedom fights, we now see the upsurge of a period of social media mutineers. These are virtually for real forcing one to ask if the Indian society is reinventing itself online? Milind Deora, a young politician from the Congress, insists we as a society need to be vary of this. 'The number of Twitter followers, Facebook likes, and TRP ratings are being naively used as proxies for popularity and approval ratings. It threatens to cultivate an unfettered, noisy, and sometimes meaningless discourse culture with "famous" personalities pontificating on everything, so as to be seen as "speaking out".'[2]

What do these increasing bursts of outrage and public display of views on networking websites signify? Is there a political bone in every Indian? Are we beginning to experience a new kind of democratic resurrection? Or has the yearning for change awakened the beasts inside, extracted politicians' dirty laundry, and landed on clothesline of social media for all to gawk and analyse?

THE TIMING IS CRUCIAL

The world is on people's fingertips, thanks to a mobile phone revolution. Add to that the access to technological breakthroughs happening every few seconds. This easy access legitimizes the concept of 'broadcast yourself' to borrow YouTube's punch line. Isn't this the first time in human history that anyone and everyone can be heard, known, and read by the world? The right to expression and opinion is no longer just the domain of those in television studios, or authors of whitepapers. This is also evident by the number of new faces—even if self-professed—we are now seeing across different media. 'Social media has created a new idea of social. It's different. Digital has a different idea of time, speed, relationships, and the self. Yet it relates to the idea of social in a different way,' explains Shiv Vishvanathan, professor at OP Jindal University. A paper presented by Nitin Pai and Sneha Shankar of Takshashila explains, 'Technological factors—specifically the use of Internet and mobile communications —are seen as an important instrument enabling protests and activism, especially because they are less sensitive to control mechanisms traditionally employed by governments of the world.'

This technology aspect of social media evolution implies the induction of a certain demographic—the youth, the techno-savvy—into the political and social streams. It is this youth factor that's all set to play a, hitherto absent, role in politics. Editor-in-chief of IBN18 network, Rajdeep Sardesai, notes in his column, 'This is, in a sense, the Virat Kohli generation, not even the Sachin Tendulkar one: their appetite for 20-20 cricket is translated into their life goals: a generation which is aggressive, aspirational, consumerist, and impatient for change. This is an India, especially in the metros, which has only used mobiles, never seen a black and white TV, is Internet-savvy and never heard of the Soviet Union.'[3] Today it's this generation that presents itself as the new audience for politics; for civil society; for change. The young are mesmerized by such discourse, tech access, and easy reach because finally they too can be a part of social change. 'By creating new expectations in politics and consumption patterns, social media speeds up the current notions of politics in the public,' says Vishvanathan. He admits social revolutions of the recent past such as Anna Hazare, protest against Delhi gang-rape, rise of AAP and other significant events remain a 'co-production'. He points out that social media plays a critical role both in 'problem and the problem solving. The gang-rape in Delhi in December 2012 would not have created the furore it did without social media pressure.'

The Takshashila paper also highlights a number of underlying factors: youth bulge, urbanization, size of the middle-class, mobile phone penetration, and growth of social media as important triggers. It is highly likely that these factors—in various combinations—have a causal relationship with the eruption of protests. And so in many ways the sudden spillage of the vitriolic is manifested in discontent.

Social media has brought together people on high-speed engagement platforms where the word of mouth is passed on in a matter of seconds. This has meant a certain sense of unity among those with common goals and ideas or those with a common enemy. For example in India, the recent social churn is driven by discontent against ruling establishments. PR honcho Dilip Cherian agrees with this. 'This is inherently evident in the responses, it is the one platform where the outreach is possible and effective. Also it's the result of the comfort of anonymity. And other factors that are never quite talked about.'

However, Sengupta in her article explains that one needs to be wary of this rancor as the population on social networking sites cannot be considered the voice of a larger chunk of people across India. 'The problem occurs when we try to infer population beliefs from this limited sample and claim that what we see online is an accurate reflection of the "mood of the nation". This is a classic case of "selection bias"— an issue economists have been grappling with for some time now. Put simply: unlike data in science experiments, social science data is inherently biased (towards those who choose to participate) and therefore making inferences from it blindly, dangerous.'[4]

What also adds strength to Sengupta's case is that there is tremendous urge among people to act or react on social media fully aware of the fact that they are not responsible or accountable for their actions. A view or opinion doesn't make it incumbent on them to do a certain task or follow up on their revolutionary ideas as expressed on Facebook, Twitter, or any other online medium. 'The notion that computer mediated communication gives people a strategic freedom to express themselves because they are unaccountable has also been identified as a cause for the ostensible increase in anti-normative behaviour in computer mediated communication compared with face to face communication,' says a paper authored by Tom Postmes, Russell Spears, Martin Lea called 'Breaching of Building Boundaries—Side Effects of Computer Mediated Communication.'[5]

ADDICTION OF THE 'INSTANT'

It is clear that social media plays an important role in shaping thoughts in a society. People interact, share, and exchange resources through social networks. It promotes free flow of information and sharing of resources beyond boundaries. The ability to do so has altered the way ideas change hands and how fast those ideas spread. At the same time, news and any information that would usually take days or even weeks to travel from one location to another can now take place in seconds. This ease of communication has never been so available to people around the world as it is now and it is still continuing to evolve.

Ping, post, or just a blinking red light are the new knocks on people's doors. It's not necessarily limited to a certain generation. People have a constant urge to look at Facebook, update their statuses, and share their location. 'We go to the loo in the middle of the night, and we want to check whether our friends liked our posts. Whether we have more e-mail. This is the new "content sleep" I guess,' shares young Anjali Bhargav who is hooked on to social media as an aspiring journalist. As such technological changes keep people wired, the need for gratification is fast evolving and so is its nature. A recent piece in the *Sydney Morning Herald* articulated how some of the notifications, that we have got addicted to, were born. It narrates the story of 24-year-old Facebook engineer Wayne Chang who discovered 'ping'. He reportedly put on a recording device on his personal computer, pursed his lips together and recorded the popping sound he made. His colleagues made a few electronic tweaks, and just like that, the first official Facebook notification 'ping' was born. 'While technology has made it effortless to bask in good vibes, it also has fueled an unlimited source of digital gratification that competes with the rest of our life.'[6] And this is beginning to show in how we behave online. Everything is NOW.

Has social media watered down serious debates into instant noodles? All it needs is a 2-minute thought, discussion, action, and reaction? Has it put attention span in jeopardy? And are we now laying the same rules of impatience with politics and policy? Shiv Vishvanathan says that because of social media, people want to have 'activity and speed in decision-making. They don't want to wait 5 years but 5 minutes.' But this sense of quick-fix actually is embedded in a deeper thought. The notion that people are mostly political. That we are not just looking for rapidity but want to extract the idea that infects our new mentality—that of us all being 'political beings'. Did we remain dormant to this notion?

SCRATCHING THE POLITICAL SURFACE

Social media has put the spotlight on how intimate Indians are with politics. They have it in their bloodstream. 'If there is one thing every Indian is, they are political,' explains Shiv Vishvanathan. He picks the very basic unit of society—the family. 'Why think of a nation. Every family is political. All soap operas show that there is more conspiracy in the family than just at the national level. That's how inherent it is.' He admits, though many hide this well, that from bazaar, trade union to a nation or even networking—we are absolutely the most political country. 'We are deeply fractional, divisive, but united in controversy,' shares Vishvanathan.

This isn't exactly news about the Indian society. A senior cabinet minister once told me that scratch the surface and you will find most Indians are inherently communal. That's the construct in which we have built our society, he insisted. Communalism is a problem. 'And social media can sharpen it,' says Vishvanathan. 'What social media does is accentuate certain tension.' This can be witnessed by the proliferation of right-wing groups online. There is a notion that most trolls on Indian timelines are against a certain political ideology and not universally against all. Vishvanathan notes that in India, religious groups have been ahead of the curve as far as technological forces go. 'Religious groups—take the example of Sri Sri Ravi Shankar, Swami Narayan, even the RSS. How come they are the most IT-savvy groups in India? Half of Silicon Valley is religious in a way.' Getting organized and organized online is a central part of social media today. As groups with a common cause unite, they discover the most potent and well-researched way to engage the medium to its best results. 'Now add a time dimension to it—social media has contributed to the hype of the democratic imagination,' says Vishvanathan. So that takes us to the question if citizenship is going to get altered entirely as we move ahead from this base?

CITIZENSHIP IN FOR A REINVENTION?

Given that social media may be an alternative sphere for sharing views and opinions and discussing political life in any nation, we may imply that the social media can play an important role in democracy establishment, concludes Sergiv Prokhorov in his paper 'Social Media and Democracy: Facebook as a Tool for the Establishment of Democracy in Egypt'.[7] It highlights how Facebook and Twitter may now be considered a new version of a public sphere. For example, in the case of the Egyptian revolution, social media proved to be more effective and impactful than traditional media. The revolution was 'socially driven rather than hierarchically driven.' It further explains that 'political barriers between political authority and public were lifted, making it easier for citizens to contribute and make their worries heard.'

Politicians in India are becoming cognizant of this. Milind Deora, a young Member of Parliament from Congress Party, admits in a piece he wrote for the *Times of India*, 'Indian youth are organizing themselves better with the aid of technology to engage with politicians, journalists, businessmen and society at large, thus demanding better governance and increased transparency. Social media has fantastically broken down communication barriers in government-citizen relationship.' Look at this, in the run up to Lok Sabha polls, Facebook users were able to discuss the electoral agenda of country's top politicians including Narendra Modi, Mamata Banerjee, Akhilesh Yadav, Arvind Kejriwal and some others thanks to the launch of a special initiative, 'Facebook Talks Live', by the social networking website. 'We have always been focussed on making sure that we give people the power to share, and to make the world more open and connected. This and the opportunity to engage actively and regularly with constituents have led campaign teams and leaders to use the medium, making Facebook a core part of the political infrastructure in the country,' said a Facebook official. This was another great step towards collapsing walls between the government and the governed.[8]

In this and many other ways we are seeing a transformation of the idea of democracy in some ways this conclusion can be used to understand the implication of the AAP and India Against Corruption revolution in India. The levels of oppression and media gag are certainly drastically different between India and Egypt. From mobilizing crowds, lecturing new and possibly radical ideas, both IAC and AAP made a democratic impact. Taking criticism in their strike, Arvind Kejriwal took a political plunge to give democracy a chance rather than speechifying change. He won. It was a democratic victory. The years ahead expect popular support to go towards them and similar movements. With the chorus rising around change, anti-corruption drives under AAP's arrival in Delhi, many power centres, constitutional authorities, and civil servants admit that AAP's stunning political debut is not an isolated phenomenon, but part of a larger churning across India.

WHO IS IN CONTROL?

It's possibly fair to say that the Indian democratic set up has thus far held up strongly against any attempt to gag such quick-media. This was threatened though when Information Minister Kapil Sibal talked of controlling malicious content and monitoring the networking sites but he was criticized to the point where he was compelled to express wonder and amusement at the power of social media. Now he too has joined Twitter.

For democracy and citizenship to transform or remain on the path of change, it's very critical to know who maintains ownership of these networks and how; and if the government or the ruling political powers have a control over the same. 'When non-democratic governments have leverage over the content and structure of social networks, users lose the ability to access independent points of view and learn about government malfeasance. Not only is information sharing monitored and potentially blocked, but democracy activists avoid networks connected with government authorities for fear of reprisals,' says Joshua Tucker in the *Monkey Cage* while analysing countries like Russia.[9]

From an Indian perspective, while we don't yet face very significant problems of dictatorial government, we need to explore how to put social media in the driver's seat for democracy. How to retain values of free speech, without manufacturing content or consent and at the same time get the government involved in the process and engage on social media in a more material way than information spread.

This does put the subject of what's genuine for consumption on the Internet up for debate. From trolls, fakes, to the marketing power and prowess of social media, there is a lot yet to be deciphered in terms of its actual outcome. Columnist George Monbiot has a serious body of work on the underlying aspects of social media and asserts that there are several forces at work in building opinion on web. In a way, he explains, social media too 'organizes' itself to push forward a certain view. In effect, then, can social media be used to suggest a 'perceived' result? Could it cheat its consumer? 'The weapon used by both state and corporate players is a technique known as astroturfing. An astroturf campaign is one that mimics spontaneous grassroots mobilizations, but which has in reality been organized. Anyone writing a comment piece in Mandarin critical of the Chinese government, for example, is likely to be bombarded with abuse by people purporting to be ordinary citizens, upset by the slurs against their country.'[10]

The Takshashila study elucidates that today's governments operate in a hierarchical manner, top-down and bottom-up, in silos, bound by hard rules and distinct leadership. The hierarchical state can learn to handle emerging challenges but the learning process itself takes time due to the same structural reasons. This may be broadly true of the government and government-aided agencies in India as well as a general challenge to take up change. Deora suggests the role of social media should be to aid and not act upon solutions. 'Possibly the role of today's social media, maybe even digital media and news media, is in flagging issues but these may not be the right forums to solve the issues or even debate solutions. For that, we must look to other institutions—ones that are more nuanced and experienced,' he advises. The challenges—rampantly discussed on social networks—like with going back to institutions that may have betrayed citizens in underperforming duties. And this includes the Parliament where someone was heard saying that social media is now the foster home of more meaningful debates than the Parliament itself. However, the channel and structure of communication when put aside, does lead us back to the deep rooted question of changing values as media outlets and outrage spills evolve in expression.

Another interesting point is that social media relations cannot be substituted for reals ones. While participation and engagement is much more convenient online; the passion and initiative that drives an individual for a cause may be virtually missing. 'While social networks may be useful for some communication,' says author Malcolm Gladwell, 'to alert like-minded acquaintances to social events, or to solve a specific "weak tie" problem, such as the location of a bone marrow donor—they do not promote the passionate collective engagement that causes individuals to make commitments that result in social change.'[11] He further concludes, 'The evangelists of social media seem to believe that a Facebook friend is the same as a real friend. Social networks are effective at increasing participation—by lessening the motivation that participation requires. In other words, Facebook activism succeeds not by motivating people to make a real sacrifice but by motivating them to do the things that people do when they are not motivated enough to make a real sacrifice.'

So we are back to the main question—has social media led to a social churn in the fabric of our society? There is no straight answer but 'no' as an answer can be definitely eliminated. 'There were people who were badly served but didn't have a voice. There was no access to knowledge. Today information expectations are changing. All kind of classes will be able to get this open access,' explains Vishvanathan and that's something hard to turn down as an idea whose time has come.

References

1. http://www.indiasocial.in/why-social-media-can-be-so-unsocial-by-anurag-batra/

2. http://timesofindia.indiatimes.com/home/opinion/edit-page/The-social-media-cacophony/articleshow/21807821.cms

3. http://www.firstpost.com/politics/why-modi-succeeded-but-rahul-failed-in-attracting-young-india-1055125.html?utm_source=ref_article

4. http://www.criticaltwenties.in/economicsocialpolicy/
   opinion-explosion-in-indian-social-media-a-driver-for-
   real-change-or-just-a-lot-of-noise

5. http://personalpages.manchester.ac.uk/staff/martin.
   lea/papers/1998-EJ%20Postmes%20Spears%20Lea%20
   Boundaries%20CR.pdf

6. http://www.smh.com.au/digital-life/digital-life-news/
   social-media-redefines-mental-gratification-20131108-
   2x661.html

7. http://dspace.mah.se/bitstream/handle/2043/14120/
   Thesis%20Sergiy%20Prokhorov%20MU.pdf?sequence=2

8. http://economictimes.indiatimes.com/articleshow/
   30720454.cms?utm_source=contentofinterest&utm_
   medium=text&utm_campaign=cppst

9. http://themonkeycage.org/2013/05/17/social-networks-
   and-democracy/

10. http://www.monbiot.com/2010/12/13/reclaim-the-cyber-
    commons/

11. http://www.theguardian.com/books/2010/oct/03/malcolm-
    gladwell-twitter-doesnt-work

12

Social Media and a Credibility Crisis

Every person on social media is entitled to publish his opinion. While this democratic medium has many advantages, it does raise questions on whether such opinions and opinion-led discourses are credible. Has India yet to see the downside of this form of 'hot off the press'? While we know that social media has led to paradigm shifts in ways people work and do business, interact and socialize, learn and obtain knowledge, there is also this mortal fear that social media is having such an impact that it's raising questions on the quality of information sought and put out. What's rumour, and what's real? Who are the real personalities and who are fakes? With fans and followers as the new measures, is there a big question mark on the qualitative benefits of social media? Does such widespread availability of information threaten the security of the nation, states, corporations? Is this obsession of the instant leading to digital indigestion for those who are the very products of this media?

Management consultant Kamini Banga, in an interview with the author, puts the finger on the very idea of news consumption and democracy. 'Being in the public eye certainly raises the pressure and some would argue that long-term interests are abandoned in favour of short-term ones. The reach and immediacy of engagement certainly gives it the aura of a big churn. Can democracy—the 5-year wonder—survive this churn?' Does immediacy, democratic consumption of news and information, put at risk the very quality of stuff put out in public domain via social media? Are there enough checks and balances in place? Is the credibility of information now the nucleus of all challenges? Columnist George Monbiot who has a serious body of work on the underlying aspects of social media says, 'The Internet is a remarkable gift, which has granted us one of the greatest democratic opportunities since universal suffrage. We're in danger of losing this global commons as it comes under assault from an army of trolls and flacks, many of them covertly organized or trained.'[1]

One wonders if news and views and opinion on social media are a signal or noise. How much should one follow them? Are trends gamechanging in reality whether it's for government or corporations? The Internet and social media are growing both in size and complexity, as well as playing an increasing role in our lives. There are many challenges ahead and most of these put the credibility of speed and accuracy of the medium in spotlight.

Finding relevant, timely, and trustworthy content out of a barrage of irrelevant chatter remains a central issue. How can people distinguish organized and malicious attempts on social media? Sifting through and differentiating between spam and abuse? Are there vested interests at play? All these questions are relevant for the social media strategy of a business or a political party.

What worries the media advisor of our Prime Minister is the idea of anonymity that is prevalent throughout social media use. Pankaj Pachauri believes the crisis is already at the doorstep of social media for being able to mask the identity of trolls. 'Credibility crisis is already there because the basic problem in there is the anonymity. On FB you cannot be anonymous. But on Twitter and YouTube you can be hidden, in a guise and that's going to be the undoing of social media.'

With about 10 percent Internet penetration and around 90 million users engaging on networking sites—social media does punch above its weight by virtue of sheer numbers but not without enough doubts for all. While Pachauri's concern remains valid, there are more deep-rooted issues to assess as social media and Internet spread like viral across the world. And this includes the role of government in securing and supporting the data flow.

According to a detailed report by Sharinaz Ismail and Roslina Abdul Latif called 'Authenticity Issues of Social Media: Credibility, Quality and Reality', the Internet is an environment full of uncertainty and various types of players, and an online user always experiences some level of risk. Thus, trust has become the strategy for dealing with uncertain outcomes or future and it is considered one of the most reliable predictor for online behaviours.[2]

The report analyses data to conclude that the assessment of credibility in the online environment is often much more complex than in previous media contexts due to the multiplicity of sources embedded in the numerous layers of online dissemination of content. A primary concern with social media remains the sheer volume of information that is generated with little or no oversight. All these factors have led to questioning the cause and effect of social media. Among such impact is the notion of over-democratization.

A CASE OF OVER-DEMOCRATIZATION

'It's one thing to see the sausage get made. It's another thing entirely to watch the pig get slaughtered,' says Wesley Donehue, a Republican Internet consultant who teaches federal and state candidates how best to use new technologies in their campaigns. Wesley was named a GOP Innovator of the Year in 2013 by *Campaigns and Elections* magazine in the United States. 'There's a domino effect when it comes to transparency. In policy making, lots of ideas are thrown out in order to set the good apart from the bad, and in order to stake out a position for compromise.'[3]

Take the example of AAP, which came to power in Delhi with great enthusiasm. A lot of this election was driven by social media and so was the party's popularity. Arvind Kejriwal, the state's new Chief Minister (before Kejriwal resigned over the issue of the Jan Lokpal bill), had a unique way of governing and chose protest over politics in its traditional sense. Social media helped in shaping the agenda for India's largest and most important city, the national capital Delhi. It also catapulted a newly formed political party into a serious player in just over a year. But even most ardent followers of AAP have wondered if there is a thing as too much democratization and seeking of public opinion with doubtful execution capabilities. All this played out on social media and this is where the poster boy of the online generation, Kejriwal, got the maximum brickbats. He started trending for the wrong reasons, such as spending too much time discussing his austerity approach rather than getting down to real governance after being announced as Delhi's Chief Minister. In another example, in an attempt to remain transparent, Kejriwal talked of taking every decision to the citizen—citizens who expected more control and less confusion from him. For instance, Kejriwal and the Delhi police got into a serious stand-off over corruption. Delhi's police force is run by the federal government and so Kejriwal demanded the suspension of a number of policemen. The matter got out of hand and police prevented, even roughed up, a few protestors from Kejriwal's camp who were attempting to go to the Home Minister's office. Was Kejriwal—a stellar product of social media upsurge—suddenly losing all gained ground because he was in a rush to fix things? Was he naïve to think transparency would wipe out corruption over a night? Bad press came from within his supporters. Capt. G.R. Gopinath said that Kejriwal and his Cabinet should govern from their offices and only his party workers should protest. 'Demanding suspension of police personnel is missing the woods for the trees...' quoted an article in the *Times of India*.[4] 'Social and news media alleged that the party was indulging in terror tactics, questioning whether this mode of protest was to fight a social evil or to massage its own ego. The party's strategy on the issue was also questioned as it posed a threat to the security of the capital ahead of the Republic day.'

The result is a political discourse that is becoming devoid of real ideas, and instead pared down to the safest of talking points. It suddenly put into question the credibility of Kejriwal's social media campaign which projected him as a decision-maker, and a crusader of political work—something he himself seemed to struggle with.

TRANSPARENCY

What is the nature of transparency that social media can bring to governance? Are countries across the world willing to accept the changes to such free flow of information?

The famous cases of Julian Assange of Wikileaks and Edward Snowden are testimony that even the US—where the Internet proliferates through most of the population—is still uncertain on dealing with the extent of information exchange. Hasn't former US Secretary of State, Hillary Clinton, spoken openly attacking China's attempts to block Google, but yet is among those who criticized the idea of Wikileaks?

On the other hand, there are concerns around how much information should really be put out there because a lot of it is simply being offered voluntarily by people who log on to social sites. Vivek Wadhwa, in a piece written for *Washington Post* in January 2014 asserts, 'Governments don't need informers any more. Social media allows government agencies to spy on their political masters, their own citizens, in a way that would make Big Brother jealous. We record our thoughts, emotions, likes, and dislikes on Facebook; we share our political views, social preferences, and plans. We post intimate photographs of ourselves. No spy agency or criminal organization could actively gather the type of data that we voluntarily post for them.'[5]

In addition to serious efforts, there are also some rib-tickling examples to share here. AAP's Arvind Kejriwal in his quest to keep his strategy of honesty, openness, and engagement with his audience, let loose a virus on social media a day after being sworn in as Delhi's Chief Minister. From seeking way too many opinions on many governance matters in the garb of 'people's choice' to having public announcement on ablutions. The highlight of these was the tweet he sent out for missing his first big day at work as the new Chief Minister of Delhi @arvindkejriwal tweeted: Running 102 fever since yester-day. Severe loose motions. Sad that I won't be able to attend office today.

This tweet was candid enough and it sure did trigger a viral story on social media.

'How's this for a transparent CM?' tweeted @samanth_s

Another one @rachitseth tweeted: 'Loose Motions and Loose Emotions, Arvind Kejriwal and Kumar Vishwas'

LIVE BY FIRE, DIE BY FIRE

The question mark on social media, its credibility, and the pressures it carries for everyone in the public eye came to fore in a most difficult way when Sunanda Pushkar and Shashi Tharoor's marital state of affairs was brought to the microblogging site which eventually may have led to the death of Pushkar. Transparency and public display were given new meanings as Pushkar used the social media space to share her displeasure over the friendship of Tharoor with a journalist of Pakistan.

'The more information you put out there, the more vulnerable you are,' says Smita Prakash in her column for *Mid-Day*, written in the aftermath of Pushkar's death. Trinamool's Derek O' Brien had a few years ago mentioned on NDTV's We The Tweeple program, 'Twitter is like going for a picnic with a tiger where eventually the tiger eats you up.'[6]

While the book amply focusses on the positives of social media and the transparency it affords, it's important to highlight the limits of this transparency and what need not be brought under public scrutiny. The notion of openness and transparent governance has its limits and how effectively it brings solutions on board for both the government and the governed need to be analysed. Transparency also exposes loose hems around ideologies, people, public and private lives. We no longer live in a world where off record is off record. Once an issue slips into social media, it is considered on record. You are what you post. And indeed that's the ugly truth of communication in this socially, hyper-linked world. Governments in the emerging world, in countries like Russia, Brazil, India and others have a lot of work to do in changing perception about openness.

CREATING MONSTERS?

A by-product of this credibility crisis is the fact that any social media overdose is leading to completely different formats of communication that thrives on self-expression, bullying, and isolation. One wonders if it is also making monsters out of its users. Take any of the cases of Rahul Gandhi's TV interview, the Radia tapes, or Internet censorship—the Twitter world too has been at fault by not being in a position to offer any meaningful discourse and being absolved in vitriolic exchanges. Often, if not always, microblogging sites have shown a higher leaning towards defamatory and abusive attacks rather than an intelligent and cordial discussion on a political subject. Of course this is partly driven by the way the demographics play out on Twitter—where people are mostly opinionated, politically branded, and tend to participate only in controversial discussions.

Kamini Banga uses the example of Steven Pinker's work to explain this. 'The Harvard College Professor of psychology has said that given the overload of information it is a boon to have these sites that save us time and keep us connected. The reverse side of your argument is that it offers people a channel for self expression—something they never had before. Ascribing all these negative outcomes to social media is making a monster out of it.'

FAKING NEWS

A *New York Times* editorial highlights how social media can also be subject to significant abuse. Some politicians have been accused of boosting their apparent popularity on social media with legions of followers who don't exist and of using social media to smear their opponents. There have been unsubstantiated reports that social media may have been used to fan violence against religious and ethnic groups; the dissemination of a fraudulent video may have helped spark deadly clashes between Hindus and Muslims in the city of Muzaffarnagar in September 2013.

X-Index which documents issues on censorship, cites a few more examples. In 2012, false rumours spread through MMS resulted in the exodus of northeastern migrants from south India, as the threat of violence seemed imminent. At the time, the government had to ban bulk text messaging, and ultimately restrict messages to 5 a day to check more rumours. Meanwhile, with global violence in the aftermath of the YouTube video, The Innocence of Muslims, the government of Jammu and Kashmir decided to suspend the internet for a few days to prevent any incidents.[7]

Apart from such examples, social media has indeed put the spotlight on certain stories which are genuine but tend to get overshadowed. CNN-IBN's Political Editor finds social media a real hub. 'I think the credibility crisis is much lesser today than it was, say, a year back,' says Bhupendra Chaubey. 'I think people are beginning to understand the importance of social media. Recently the story of a young Arunachal boy being beaten to death became screaming front page headlines and hours of prime time TV after it came on social media first.'

IDEA OF CENSORSHIP

Closely linked to the analysis of credibility of social media is the notion of censorship. The new digital context is not simple to govern and there are several question marks on whether at all the construct of social media must be governed. Would censoring social media discourse be going against the grain of what it stands for? Openness and free flow of thoughts? Governments across the world and in India are finding ways to use filters, and possibly engage in mass surveillance, leading to Snowden-style concerns across the post-modern communication community.

At one time, civil rights had a run-in against social media when two young girls in Mumbai were arrested for criticizing the traffic shutdown due to a bandh called by Shiv Sena. The incident reignited the debate over free speech in the country and put the spotlight on social media and the laws that can govern it. The girls were booked under section 295(a) of the IPC for hurting religious sentiments and section 66(a) of the Information Technology Act, 2000.[8] By this logic, practically every individual making politically incorrect comments on social media would be liable for arrest? And so the discourse on the laws began.

During their learning curve, politicians in India had messed up their approach to social media. Information Minister Kapil Sibal had said in 2011—when he had not joined Twitter himself—that the government would introduce guidelines to ensure 'blasphemous material' did not appear on the Internet. 'The print media is subject to the laws of this country, the electronic media is subject to the laws of this country. My only question is why should social media not be a subject?' he famously asked. This was perhaps a reflection of the fact that the government has been unable to keep pace with a fast-unfolding social media revolution, unable to deal with its unbridled power and reach. Two years later, in 2013, Sibal admitted, 'It's a new medium, it's an evolving medium. We don't know how to deal with it ourselves. We need to understand the power of the social media.'

Sibal's contemporary P. Chidambaram had earlier acknowledged the power of social media and mobs. 'Flash mob is a new phenomenon...sometimes they gather to dance and sing. But sometimes they gather to protest... I don't think we are fully prepared to deal with it.'[9]

Politics and social media will both face challenges going forward. As politicians learn to use the medium to favour them during elections, there will be an effort to break formats, try new campaigns, and expose themselves to praise and criticism. Donahue articulates this. 'As the use of social media accelerates, it's incumbent upon everyone involved in the political process to make sure its power is used to harness everything good about the American political system, rather than to hasten political trends that are hurting our republic.' Clearly, this holds true about the Indian political scene as well. Credibility of social media will remain a subject of debate for years to come but at the same time it will not stop the experiment of testing politics in the online world.

References

1. http://www.monbiot.com/2010/12/13/reclaim-the-cyber-commons/

2. http://www.academia.edu/2579304/Authenticity_Issues_of_Social_Media_Credibility_Quality_and_Reality

3. http://edition.cnn.com/2012/04/24/opinion/donehue-social-media-politics/

4. http://timesofindia.indiatimes.com/city/delhi/Dwindling-support-bad-press-forced-Arvind-Kejriwal-to-end-stir/articleshow/29173823.cms

5. http://www.washingtonpost.com/blogs/innovations/wp/2014/02/03/10-years-after-facebook-social-media-is-only-beginning-to-shake-up-the-world/

6. http://www.youtube.com/watch?v=f5ICO6OeX0M

7. http://www.indexoncensorship.org/2013/10/india-social-media/

8. http://www.dnaindia.com/mumbai/report-anti-thackeray-fb-post-two-girls-arrested-for-bandh-comments-get-bail-1766830

9. http://www.politicalpast.com/P._Chidambaram/2012/12/

Conclusion

At the rate social media is permeating our lives—our gathering of information and our decisions—the day can't be far when it may be credited for a political win. In the case of AAP, Narendra Modi and Barack Obama, there have been several examples documented to suggest networking sites proved their worth and contribution to political mileage. A post that can change the voter's mood? A tweet that reflectsa politician in good light? Internet and social media are becoming leading influencers behind who gets elected and how. We are now certain that social media will have a definite impact on elections simply because of its power of influence.

'The use of social media in today's campaign is not only important—it is critical,' says Hubert 'Sonny' Massey, a business instructor and advisor at South University, Savannah. 'Millions of people are involved in using social networks daily. It is the opportunity to be in touch with large numbers of voters quickly, constantly, and at a low cost.'[1]

The 'viral thumb', as someone called it, is changing how we consume information and, therefore, the choices we make. And that means it's also changing the way we choose our leaders. Our digital fingers have for once helped in creating a level playing field, allowing people of different walks of life to participate and influence the decision of who will govern us. The surge in mobile phone usage, proliferation of basic phones with social media apps, and an overall push for further internet connectivity makes India an exciting market for socio-political trends using the web.

India remains at the cusp of change when it comes to technology and communication and tends to pick on trends ahead of the curve. For example, India straight hopped to the mobile phone concept giving landlines a complete skip. It's not different with social media and its impact. Social networks make the world into a 'global village' a term popularized by Marshall McLuhan in his books *The Gutenberg Galaxy: The Making of Typographic Man* and *Understanding Media*. McLuhan's prescription was that internet was an 'extension of consciousness' and the globe contracted into a village by electric technology, brings all social and political functions together in a sudden implosion, electric speed heightening human awareness of responsibility to an intense degree.

Let's look at the example of the Middle East uprisings, now known as Arab Spring, when thousands of people got together to protest against dictatorial governments of north Africa and Arab region. The impact was so widespread that former US security advisor Mark Pfeiflesaid in 2009 that Twitter was instrumental in helping document the crisis in Iran following the contested presidential election results. Social media became a window to the world. 'When traditional journalists were forced to leave the country, Twitter became a window for the world to view hope, heroism, and horror,' he said. 'It became the assignment desk, the reporter, and the producer. And, because of this, Twitter and its creators are worthy of being considered for the Nobel Peace Prize,' he wrote in the *Christian Science Monitor*.[2]

The sheer richness and diversity of information available on the web is empowering people with significant knowledge. In 2006, the *Time* magazine put out a prophetic cover, albeit then reflecting the power of the few social tools of the internet and how its power to connect people would herald change. The cover put 'You' as the Person of the Year. 'It's about the cosmic compendium of knowledge Wikipedia and the million-channel people's network YouTube and the online metropolis MySpace. It's about the many wresting power from the few and helping one another for nothing and how that will not only change the world, but also change the way the world changes.' Today, these tools have multiplied from Wiki, MySpace to Facebook, Twitter, Pinterest, Vine and many more.

Users are no longer limited to one source of news. Everyone with information to share is a journalist, every other person an editor. A smartphone can be your mega studio. *Time* magazine further articulated the changing nature of the World Wide Web as one beyond the one Tim Berners Lee put together. 'The new Web is a very different thing. It's a tool for bringing together the small contributions of millions of people and making them matter. Silicon Valley consultants call it Web 2.0, as if it were a new version of some old software. But it's really a revolution.'[3]

The social, economic, and political repercussions of this evolving change in the web and its instruments is turning a new media tide. It has led to a new relationship between new and traditional media. Television broadcast, newspapers, and magazines continue to graze social sites for news triggers and social media becomes a great ground for scouting reactions. The catchment has significantly increased. This has not only changed how we consume news but how we produce it to. 'One specific innovation that is going to shake up everything,

I think a lot of things are going to be on digital format—for example, where are people watching videos, are they watching on standard television or watching on apps or are they watching them online?'[4]

The relationship between social media and politics also has its nodes in the desire for change. Today, the public at large is using its information and networking access to find solutions. Can civil society with their rising frustration about political apathy really channel the concept and use of social media to drive real change? Filmmaker Shekhar Kapur says on his blog, 'Like ideas, social media will give rise to communities that will rise and fall around ideas, while some will grow massively. No longer limited by geography or language, fiercely loyal communities that will go beyond commitment to nation states and form around ideals.' And these can be game-breaking or game-making for politicians.

However, despite its massive reach and power, the new sphere of influence under social media forewarns its origins lie in marketing. The ideas of organized groups on the webare presented like clockwork, strategies and efforts to sometimes brainwash people push pre-determined ideas and thoughts. It is only here that the saffron brigade can bombardtweeple with 'manufactured' information in a bid to manipulate votes. Politicians can paint a glorified story with little fact check. Views of a few can be projected as 'public opinion'. The rush for instant consumption can compromise credibility of the news received. Elections make for a particular interesting time for all such tenets to get tested, abused, and used.

While India runs the litmus test on social media through a colourful and wide net of politics during elections, there are some who speculatestill if social media is only a temporary phase? That this obsession with fans will wear off? Could it be a kind of technological coma and not an end in itself? Or does its instant nature warn of an impending death and overdose of networking-busyness forcing people to withdraw from this virtual world? Malcolm Gladwell, renowned author doesn't quite see social media as a tipping point. Gladwell says, 'While social networks may be useful for some communication—to alert like-minded acquaintances to social events, or to solve a specific 'weak tie' problem, such as the location of a bone marrow donor—they do not promote the passionate collective engagement that causes individuals to make commitments that result in social change.' But then there are those who disagree with Gladwell.

Social media will alter our world, and the signs are visible already. Technology will leapfrog, engulfing you and me in a wave that is transforming the world of media and communications. Think back to the days when mobile phones were a novelty and you never thought it would change your life. Social media is today in that phase. I would be scared if I were off the network simply because the nature of the beast is not at peaceunless you are on it. When you marry political campaigning to the power of communication of social media to connect to voters, many vistas open up. It has some real power to spur choice, turn virtual relationships into real, pit one politician against another, test the communication skills of a leader, transform global media and present an opportunity to use the internet for change. If this change takes place in the world's largest democracy with one of the youngest demographics, it truly sets the stage for a massive explosion better known as social media revolution.

References

1. http://source.southuniversity.edu/political-campaigns-and-social-media-tweeting-their-way-into-office-106986.aspx

2. http://www.telegraph.co.uk/technology/twitter/5768159/Twitter-should-win-Nobel-Peace-Prize-says-former-US-security-adviser.html

3. http://www.theguardian.com/books/2010/oct/03/malcolm-gladwell-twitter-doesnt-work

4. http://www.exchange4media.mobi/Story.aspx?news_id=54020&section_id=69#sthash.Kjr4VkB4.dpuf

Acknowledgements

The idea of writing this book emerged from a debate, over lunch with a friend, on whether social media is at the centre of politics in today's world. We met after exchanging Facebook messages. Our opinions were a cauldron of what we post and the people who influence our timelines. Several counter points and disagreements led to the birth of this book, in the quest of gauging just how much impact social media can really have. *The Big Connect*, therefore, owes it to many people for its coming into existence.

I must thank the many political leaders who joined social media and made it a most exciting medium to analyse before election 2014. Without their sense of adventure, hunger to grow their fan base (by hook or by crook), political incorrectness, and reaction to every action, this book wouldn't have found its very trigger. I would also like to thank the opinionators (opinion makers and opinion terminators) for making social media an echo chamber of honest, sometimes vitriolic viewpoints for and against politicians.

Who knew this book would become such an exciting venture and so I must thank all the special guests who took time out to speak to me about social media politics. I have been fortunate to assimilate information and data from diverse sources such as newspaper articles, academic papers, government documents, journals, books, and the Internet— all of which helped to make this book more comprehensive and richer in context.

No acknowledgments can be complete without mentioning my lovely editor, Radhika Marwah who helped make this book infinitely more readable and the entire team of Random House India.

Writing can be a rather erratic exercise and so I would like to thank my husband Shivnath for being around, accepting me with all the misgivings of my creative stream. And for questioning and debating my hypothesis on social media. I'd like to thank young Abeer, with whom I was pregnant throughout the writing of this book. A special thanks to our families for being—among other things—the guinea pigs for my questions, surveys and experiments on social media and sharing a lay person's feedback on political campaigns. And most importantly, a special mention for Maa who sends me her blessings from the stars.

A Note on the Author

Shaili Chopra is an award-winning journalist who has specialized in business reporting and is a keen watcher of developments in social media.

She was presented the Ram Nath Goenka Award for the best in business journalism for 2010-11 and the News Television Award for Best Reporter in 2007. She is among the most recognized and trusted faces in Indian journalism. She is known for breaking news and her incisive interviewing style with people like Warren Buffett, Steve Ballmer, Amartya Sen, P. Chidambaram, among others. Shaili has spent over a decade in television with organizations like ET NOW, NDTV, and CNBC. Industry chamber FICCI conferred upon her their Young Leader Award. CNN-IBN counted her among the 30 witty, intelligent women to follow on Twitter.

The Big Connect is her second book.